CHAPLAINS

OF THE BIBLE

Carol,
May God give you
all the love of heaven
for serving out great
nation. Dick
Chaplains: +
Pat
Well done good + faithful servant.

ENDORSEMENTS

"In these pages Dick and Pat Geyer go to the roots of the claim that helping people in time of need is the chief task of the Christian church. They find these roots both in history and in theology. Dick and Pat do a beautiful job explaining that the comfort we share is directly related to our awareness of God's comfort in our lives. Explore the ways He ministers to you so that you can share His comforts with others in need."

—Kim Gee, D.Min., Senior Pastor, Winfield Bible Church, Woodbine, Maryland. Disaster Service Responder for the American Red Cross, member Red Cross Speaker's Bureau.

"*Chaplains of the Bible* brings a delightful insight of chaplaincy to encourage those of us who are in the field already and an inside view of what we do to those not familiar. As a senior law enforcement chaplain and crisis intervention specialist, I appreciate how Dick and Pat have brought forward the scriptural concepts of chaplaincy and plugged them into the relevancy of our culture and times.

The greatest example of a chaplain was Jesus. He met the needs of the people "outside the walls of the church," thus enabling Him to touch the lives of people right where they were. *Chaplains of the Bible* gives us a smorgasbord of stories with an opportunity to move you to making a difference in the lives of those around you. Total 'THUMBS UP!'"

—*Mindy Albright, WVM DK (Wife and Veteran Mom, Daughter of the King) Ordained Senior Chaplain and Lead Trainer, International Fellowship of Chaplains; Disaster Response Chaplain; Approved Critical Incident Stress Management Instructor and Advanced Group Instructor, International Critical Incident Stress Foundation; Madison Heights (MI) Police Department Chaplain.*

"In all my training experience, I have never seen such a well-written, easy-to-read book, fully devoted to biblical perspectives for chaplains. What better resource than the Bible, with practical real-life stories that amplify and highlight principles of conduct for chaplains and 'care givers' in many and varied circumstances."

—*Chuck Duby, Senior Chaplain, Hope Force International; Board-certified Christian Crisis Response Chaplain with the American Association of Christian Counselors, recipient of International Critical Incident Stress Foundation Certificate of Specialized Training in Pastoral Crisis Intervention, Ordained Minister, International Missions career for 22 years, visiting over 40 countries. Hope Force International, based in Nashville, Tennessee, trains and deploys the Christian community in advance to compassionately respond to those in crisis from disasters and chronic need. Hope Force provides a clear pathway of service, meeting practical, emotional, and spiritual needs of those served.*

CHAPLAINS

OF THE BIBLE

Inspiration for Those Who Help Others in Crisis

RICHARD E. GEYER & PATRICIA M. GEYER

AMBASSADOR INTERNATIONAL
GREENVILLE, SOUTH CAROLINA & BELFAST, NORTHERN IRELAND

www.ambassador-international.com

Chaplains of the Bible
Inspiration for Those Who Help Others in Crisis

Printed in the United States of America

Print Edition: 978-1-62020-029-2
Electronic Edition: 978-1-62020-030-8

Cover Illustration, Cover Design and Page Layout by Matthew Mulder

AMBASSADOR INTERNATIONAL
Emerald House
427 Wade Hampton Blvd.
Greenville, SC 29609, USA
www.ambassador-international.com

AMBASSADOR BOOKS
The Mount
2 Woodstock Link
Belfast, BT6 8DD, Northern Ireland, UK
www.ambassador-international.com

The colophon is a trademark of Ambassador

CONTENTS

FOREWORD

GOD IS MOBILIZING AN EVER-GROWING army of faith-based chaplains to serve a new generation of desperate, hurting people. These are the victims of unprecedented natural and man-made disasters, beginning with those who were devastated by the September 11, 2001 attacks on our nation and continuing on with record-breaking hurricanes, tornadoes, floods, earthquakes, wildfires, mass shootings, and more—including economic trauma. Chaplains are confronting challenges—in the United States and elsewhere—that are without parallel in scope, complexity, and risk.

Traditional chaplain work continues, but we are called to move beyond those roles to meet the deepest spiritual (and other) needs of large numbers of people who are homeless, hungry, and hurting. It is the nature of the times, a "new normal" for chaplains and all of society.

Organizations that equip, certify, and sponsor chaplains—such as the International Fellowship of Chaplains—are ramping up their training programs to prepare chaplains to meet contemporary needs. Today's chaplains are blessed to have a variety of reference materials that help us do our God-ordained work. We have books, training manuals, pamphlets, and other written resources—plus a growing library of DVDs and other audio-visual materials. All these references provide chaplains with practical and timely information and advice.

These materials are "must haves" for the chaplain. But the single best resource for us may not be on the standard chaplain's reading list. It is not a recent publication; it is the book that has served Christians through the centuries with practical advice and inspiration, providing hope and comfort, guidance, and example. It is, of course, the Bible. This ageless Word of God not only tells us how to live our lives as Christians. It also guides us as chaplains through the fog of crisis where clear answers cannot be found without supernatural direction. On one level, the Bible leads us to the deepest understanding of how chaplains can minister to those who are under the most profound stress. On another, it guides us step by step as we deploy to deal with real world problems. The words of the Bible energize chaplains to bring spiritually-based relief and hope for a new life to those who have lost so much, even their perspective on a loving God.

Dick and Pat Geyer have done an excellent job of capturing the essence of the Bible's many messages to chaplains, embedded in the accounts of biblical chaplains as they served others while serving the Lord. The stories they trace invite us to participate vicariously in the experiences of chaplains whose accomplishments were worthy of being recorded in the Book of all Books. Their "thoughts for chaplains" draw from the stories' valuable principles that we can apply daily in our chaplain endeavors. They show how those principles were applied in biblical episodes and how we can follow them in our own experiences.

The words Dick and Pat have written speak to my heart as a chaplain. The very readable style they use allows one to read the book with ease. I trust that the words of the book will speak to you as you undertake your ministry "for such a time as this" (Esther 4:14).

One final, important word. The stories described and basic concepts identified in this book will—like the training IFOC provides—be useful not only to those who are formally designated as chaplains. The book will also enlighten and encourage those many other Christians who, from time to time, have the opportunity to help others who are in need—outside of the four walls of the church building, in the communities where they live. It will speak to those who are interested in becoming chaplains, because it describes what chaplains do and what is required of them. Finally, pastors, Bible teachers, and other church leaders will find this book to be a valuable instrument in enhancing their churches' outreach activities.

This book is a most timely resource for this era of unprecedented disasters.

David C. Vorce, Ed D., MCC
President and CEO
Senior Chaplain – Major General
International Fellowship of Chaplains

Saginaw, Michigan
May 2012

Senior Chaplain David C. Vorce is a 35-year veteran in ministry. He has served as an evangelist, pastor, and a chaplain. Chaplain Vorce is a proud father of six children, a former U.S. Marine, a psychiatric nurse, and a retired lieutenant with the Saginaw County (Michigan) Sheriff's Department. He also served twenty years as a police chaplain.

The International Fellowship of Chaplains (IFOC) is a nonprofit organization that provides training, recognition, certification, and information in the varied areas of chaplaincy. IFOC also interfaces with the secular and ministry worlds for the purpose of promoting tolerance and understanding, as well as providing professional, trained, and dedicated chaplains in the various fields of need.

PREFACE

"A chaplain is one who ministers in the workplace, serving those who are in distress. Chaplains typically meet secular as well as spiritual needs of those served."[1]

DISTRESSED PEOPLE ARE ALL AROUND us. Victims of natural and manmade disasters get a lot of attention. But we see personal tragedies every day: the friend who loses his job due to tough economic times, the family next door whose teenager takes her own life, the loved one just diagnosed with a life-threatening disease.

There is great opportunity for us to help others who are in trauma, to glorify God, and to spread the gospel in circumstances when people are receptive to His Word.

The Bible offers inspiration and guidance to those who want to be better prepared to serve the distressed. This book presents some of that divine direction, drawn from the experiences of biblical characters who aided others who were in trouble. These people served as chaplains, by the definition written above. Their

---

1   Adapted from materials prepared by the International Fellowship of Chaplains.

experiences are relevant to us because they faced circumstances and issues similar to those encountered today by those who help others in distress. As Solomon wrote, "there is nothing new under the sun" (Ecclesiastes 1:9).

Thus, the purpose of this book is to tell the biblical stories from a chaplain's perspective, connect them with the experiences of contemporary care givers, and offer thoughts for you to consider as you serve others. We offer a collection of principles for helping the distressed, with confidence that the principles are based on the authority of time-tested truths found in the Bible.

The Bible has many anecdotes of chaplains in action. So it was easy to find a dozen chaplain stories, which are featured in the first twelve chapters. A collection of vignettes from the ministry of the perfect chaplain, our Lord Jesus Christ, comprises the last chapter. Some of the biblical personalities identified as chaplains in this book are better known as leaders (Moses, chapter 8; Nehemiah, chapter 11) or as prophets (Elisha, chapter 6; Elijah, chapter 7). We may not think of these men as chaplains, but their experiences serving people in distress offer much in the way of biblical wisdom to guide us.

Who Will Benefit from This Book

Christian chaplains. It is our hope—and expectation—that this book will be a source of encouragement and motivation for those who bear the title "chaplain." Chaplains serve in all segments of our society—from disaster sites to corporate environments, battlefields to hospitals and hospices, police and fire stations to prisons. Despite widely ranging assignments and diverse backgrounds, chaplains have many challenges and experiences in common. It follows that today's chaplains can benefit by studying the experiences of biblical chaplains.

Other Christians who have a heart for helping people. Many Christians, because of circumstances, have opportunities to minister to people who are in distress. Those who do so are not chaplains in the formal sense, but nevertheless are provided—through divine intervention, perhaps—with the privilege of serving others outside the church. The encounters are typically spontaneous rather than being the result of assignment or position, but often provide opportunities to serve in a way that meets our definition of "chaplain," above. Many of the times we use the word "chaplain" in this book, we include the ordinary Christian—perhaps a member of a missions ministry or an outreach initiative, or simply one who wants to leave the church pew to serve God by serving others in need.

The training and certification of one who has the formal title of chaplain is not required to provide needed care in many situations. Anyone with a reasonable degree of emotional and spiritual maturity, and a heart for serving others, can be of assistance to someone who is hurting. Obviously, many situations require the expertise and access privileges of one who is trained, certified, and sponsored as a chaplain. In some cases, the appropriate assistance may be to help the distressed person connect with a chaplain, ordained minister, or mental health professional.

Those interested in becoming qualified chaplains. The book describes a wide range of chaplain experiences and shows what it takes—in terms of character traits, training, and endurance—to be a chaplain. So the book will be instructive for those who are thinking about becoming chaplains.

Church leaders and Bible teachers. The book will be a valuable resource for church leaders who see the opportunities for service to the distressed in their communities and who recognize—as Pastor Kim Gee stated—"that helping people in time of need is the chief task of the Christian Church." There are many opportunities to minister to people outside the four walls of the church; where that is happening, we say that "the church has left the building." Bible study leaders will find the book to be a useful resource (see the next paragraph), as will those who lead mission trips and disaster relief efforts.

Using this book

This book can be a quick read for the busy person, because it is short and in story format. But with its many references to Scripture, the book also offers a starting point for in-depth study. The book is an excellent resource for group Bible study. We learned, by teaching classes based on the book, that the biblical narratives highlighted in this book adapt well to group study. So we have included a guide for such study in an appendix. The guide's questions are designed to reinforce the concepts discussed in each chapter, elicit stories of relevant experiences from the study participants, and facilitate the transition from reading and discussing to applying. The book chapters will fit a 13-week Bible study format.

Prayer is often the beginning and ending of ministry to the needy. Because of its importance, we have included a separate appendix on prayer.

A Challenge to the Reader

These are times of peril but also times of great challenge and opportunity for those who are prepared to serve others in their hour of greatest need. These are times that require the application of God's wisdom as taught in the stories presented in this book. Paul, one of our chaplains, wrote, "Be careful how you walk, not as unwise men, but as wise, making the most of your time, because the days are evil."[2] Chaplains are called "for such a time as this" (see the story of Esther in chapter 12). It is a time to follow carefully the examples set by the model chaplain (chapter 13), who spoke of the urgency of the chaplain's work when He said, "We must work the works of Him who sent Me as long as it is day; night is coming when no one can work."[3]

May the words of this book offer encouragement and guidance to you as you set about your godly work in an era of uncertainty that nevertheless offers the opportunity to glorify the God who authored the stories presented in this book.

I thank Christ Jesus our Lord, who has strengthened me, because He considered me faithful, putting me into service.

1 Timothy 1:12

---

2   Ephesians 5:15, 16

3   John 9:4

ACKNOWLEDGEMENTS

THIS BOOK WOULD NOT HAVE been completed without the help and support of my coauthor—my wife and companion, Patricia. Pat's insights as a disaster relief chaplain and as a crisis intervention specialist were invaluable as we attempted to sort out the aspects of the biblical stories that were most relevant to the contemporary chaplain experience. She carefully read several drafts of each of the chapters, offering many useful suggestions for changes. And she provided strong support for following the project to its conclusion.

We are grateful to Mindy Albright, ordained senior chaplain and trainer for the IFOC, and Judy Vorce, IFOC senior chaplain, for their encouragement in the completion of the book. Special thanks go to Senior Chaplain Dr. Keith A. Robinson, Commander of the Houston Regional Community Chaplain Corps, for sharing his experience as a chaplain. And credit goes to many other chaplains and chaplain-trainers whose knowledge and insights—shared in classrooms, conversations, and elsewhere—helped shape the structure and form the content of this book.

This book would not have been started but for the suggestion of Dr. David Vorce, IFOC president. Pat and I were looking for biblical examples to study and follow in our chaplain work, so I asked Dr. Vorce if he knew of a book on chaplains of the Bible.

After reflecting for a moment he asked, "Why don't you write one?" After my own moment of thought, I responded "okay." Pat agreed. And the book resulted. A special "thank you" goes to Dr. Vorce for writing the foreword—and for setting a high standard for us through his years of work in a number of different roles in addition to his teaching.

This book would not have included some of the key insights that it offers had it not been for the contributions of two special groups of people. The first group—members of a number of different churches in our community—put aside other things they might have done on some summer Sunday afternoons in 2009 to participate in a Bible study that covered most of the stories that are featured in this book. The second group includes members of the Winfield Bible Chapel congregation, who attended "Chaplains of the Bible" classes in 2010 and 2011. All these people know the Bible and were able to offer key points that had not occurred to Pat and me.

Finally, this book would not have been written without the inspiration of the God who authored the stories that are retold in this book. The motivation that came through His Spirit—and the many prayers of His saints— made the writing easy and most satisfying.

Dick Geyer
May 2012

Chapter 1

THE HEART OF A CHAPLAIN: WHO IS A CHAPLAIN'S NEIGHBOR?

The Good Samaritan

Luke 10:25-37

You shall love the Lord your God with all your heart, and with all your soul, and with all your strength, and with all your mind; and your neighbor as yourself (Luke 10:27).

A CERTAIN MAN WAS TRAVELING—WHY, WE are not told, but we can surmise that he was on a short business trip. His transportation of choice was a donkey as he traveled on the road from Jerusalem down to Jericho.

The road to Jericho was "down" because the elevation dropped 3,300 feet in the 17-mile route to Jericho, situated in the Jordan River valley some 800 feet below sea level and a mere ten miles from the Dead Sea.

Because the road went downhill, the ride was easier. The hard part was negotiating safely through the winding road's rocky areas that provided hiding places for men who were a threat to travelers—robbers who gave the route the unwelcoming title "The Way of Blood."

As he moved along, our traveler came face to face with the reason for the road's reputation. Lying on the side of the road was a man who had been surrounded by thieves who had robbed him, stripped him of his clothes, beat him, and left him on the roadside, half dead.

The traveler had a choice. He could continue on his trip and get to Jericho on his schedule (maybe by nightfall—we don't know how many miles per hour a donkey could do going downhill) and leave the rescue task for someone else. Others, including two members of the religious establishment of the day, had passed by without helping. One was a priest who undoubtedly was familiar with the passage in Leviticus 19:18 ("love your neighbor as yourself") and who saw the man but stayed on the other side of the road. Another was a Levite, a temple assistant who took a close look at the man but went on his way without assisting. Both were likely traveling to Jerusalem to do their duties in the temple, and they may have reasoned, "I can't get to Jerusalem in time if I stop to help," thinking, "I am to love my neighbor *except when I have a schedule to keep.*" It seems that the man was naked, and that may have embarrassed them as well.

Our traveler's other choice was to stop and help the injured man. The compassion he felt when he saw the man lying there—his heart went out to the man—guided his decision. He chose to help. That choice earned him a title that would be passed down through the centuries and that would influence countless others to do similar acts of neighborly love—"The Good Samaritan."

The Good Samaritan poured oil and wine on the man's wounds, bandaged him (likely using his own linen), put him on his donkey, and brought him to an inn where he took care of him. The next day, he gave the innkeeper two denarii[4] and asked him to look after the man, adding, "Whatever more you spend, when I return I will repay you."

This story, told by Jesus and recorded in the Gospel of Luke, is traditionally known as a parable, although it may actually have been a true story. Either way, the story made Jesus' point to a Jewish lawyer who had demanded to know "who is my neighbor?" when confronted with the commandment, "love your neighbor as yourself." After telling the story Jesus asked, "Which one of these men proved to be a neighbor to the injured man?" The lawyer had to admit, "The one who showed mercy." Jesus' final words to him were "go and do the same."

Thoughts for the Chaplain

Compassion is at the heart of ministering to those in distress. The priest passed by the hurting man without stopping to help. So did the Levite. But the Good Samaritan took care of the helpless man. The difference? The Good Samaritan was moved by compassion. We do not know the source of his compassion. But, for the Christian, compassion follows from devotion to God. That is, loving the Lord with all our heart, soul, strength, and mind leads to loving our neighbor as ourselves. This may have been one of

---

4   A denarius was equivalent to a day's pay.

the lessons that Jesus intended the lawyer to learn from the story
He told.

One does not have to be a chaplain to serve others in appropriate cir-
cumstances. Most likely the Good Samaritan did not have chaplain
training. But when he saw the injured man, his compassion led him
to do what meets our definition of a chaplain: he ministered in the
workplace, helping someone in distress. Opportunities often arise
for Christians who are not chaplains to do the same, where the need
is immediate and no one with professional qualification is present.
Those with chaplain training can be of greater assistance in many
situations, and chaplain credentials permit access to restricted areas
that are not accessible to others. But those without such training
and credentials—motivated by compassion and guided by knowledge of Christian principles, God's leading, and common sense—
can minister to needy people when the opportunity arises.

Who is my neighbor? For our purposes, the question is "who am
I obligated to assist?" We may think of a "neighbor" as one living
next to us, someone we know—or, at the furthest reach, one living
in our local community. But Jesus did not so limit the term. In the
story, the neighbor was not only unknown to the Good Samaritan
but, far more significantly, likely was a Jew. The Jews despised and
mistreated the Samaritans, who were a mixed race that included
Gentile blood.

The Good Samaritan could have reasoned, "My neighbor is
anyone who is not a Jew, so here is my chance to get even for past
discrimination by ignoring this injured man." But his compassion
drove him to minister to one that others passed by. The hypocrisy
of the two "passers by" cannot be illustrated more strongly than

by the fact that they failed to help one of their own. The Good Samaritan did as much for a person from a hostile race as he might have done for a friend or family member—or would have wanted to have done for himself.

Jesus did not put any limits—geographic, ethnic, or other—on the definition of "neighbor." Who is a chaplain's neighbor? Anyone in distress, regardless of who the person is: friend or enemy, rich or poor, young or old, male or female, from the chaplain's ethnic group or from another.

We're not obligated to "be a neighbor" in every circumstance. We have all experienced this scenario: We are driving along the road, we see a vehicle stopped on the shoulder, and we can see that something is wrong. Should we stop and offer to help? Thoughts run through our minds: If we stop, will we be able to get to our appointment on time? Will we be safe? Is it someone who might be hostile or someone I'd rather not help? Will someone else stop to help?

No one would say that each of us should stop to help in every occasion, especially if the situation does not appear safe. Chaplains are admonished not to become "part of the problem"—that is, we are not to put ourselves in a situation where our need to be rescued or treated would add to the first responders' challenges. Stopping to help isn't the only way to respond; consider the three P's: "Pull over, call the Police for help, or Pray for the stranded motorists." Each of these actions would, in appropriate circumstances, be chaplain-like acts of compassion.

In the end, how we put our compassion into action should be guided by common sense and God's direction. However, in some circumstances what God tells us to do may involve risk; the Good Samaritan risked attack when he stopped to help the man.

Individually, we may or may not respond to a particular need. But collectively, Christians represent God's "toolbox" to meet human needs through chaplain-like outreach. As an individual, I may have a low score for mercy on the spiritual gift test, and I might think that this excludes me from chaplaincy. But consider this: I might be able to use my gift of administration to help a hurricane victim comply with government procedures for obtaining help. By using my gift, I act in a manner that is as compassionate as the action of one who administers to the physical or spiritual needs of a person injured in that same hurricane.

What does it mean to love my neighbor as myself? As He often did, Jesus turned the lawyer's question around. The lawyer asked, "Who is my neighbor?" After telling the story, Jesus turned the question to, "who *proved* to be a neighbor?" That is, who acted as a neighbor? The focus was no longer on who is to be served, but who is challenged to serve.

Furthermore, the new question showed the importance of *action*. That day, the Samaritan did more than read Scripture in the temple or say "be healed" to the man and walk on by.[5] He literally walked the talk by walking to the inn while the injured man rode the donkey. The Good Samaritan was the Golden Rule in action.[6] In the phrase, "Love your neighbor as yourself," the word "love" is

---

5   See James 2:15-17

6   "So in everything, do to others what you would have them do to you, for this sums up the Law and the Prophets." Matthew 7:12 (New International Version, NIV)

an action word. Matthew Henry wrote that the Good Samaritan's compassion spurred him to loving action: "when he drew out his soul, he reached forth his hand."[7] That is, when he called on the compassion that was in his soul, he was compelled to reach out to help the man.

"Loving his neighbor" also meant that the Good Samaritan gave the best of what he had, starting with his time. He poured his oil and wine on the wounds and likely used his own linen to bind the wounds. He gave the equivalent of two days' wages for the man's care and promised more if needed. Here is a contemporary example of giving your best: During the summer and fall, Dick provides produce from his garden and orchard to needy families who live in our county. At first, he gave mostly the "leftovers"—the blemished and older produce. Then God showed him that what He wanted was the opposite: the best goes to the needy. Now, he calls his produce ministry "First Fruits"[8]—and Pat teases him about getting the "leftovers"! (She does get enough of the best to meet our needs.)

Opportunities to minister come unexpectedly and not necessarily at the most convenient time. The Good Samaritan was not on a mission trip in response to a call from God (or his church). He was probably not looking for someone to help as he entered each bend in the highway. He was just going about his business as he came to the decision point on the road. When he chose to stop and serve, his schedule most likely was interrupted; had he not stopped, he may well have

---

7   Matthew Henry's Commentary on the Whole Bible (World Bible Publishers, Iowa Falls, IA, not copyrighted) Vol. V, p. 687

8   "You shall bring the choice first fruits of your soil into the house of the Lord your God" (Exodus 23:19).

reached Jericho that same day. But he chose the stranger's comfort over his own convenience.

Pat was really excited about the first day of the "Chaplains of the Bible" study we started in our community. She loves the story of the Good Samaritan, and she looked forward to sharing her experiences as a chaplain with the others. Then she received a call to go to a city that had been devastated by a tornado, and she would need to leave the morning of the day of our first Bible study. She was very disappointed—but she chose to go where she was able to put some of the lessons from the Good Samaritan story into action. And God blessed her with experiences that she is able to share with others, experiences that she would not have had if she had stayed home.

Provision for follow-up care can be crucial. The man had not recovered from his wounds by the next morning. The Good Samaritan needed to move on from the inn but did not do so until he took action to assure that the man would be cared for. To make sure that this would happen, he left money with the innkeeper and promised more if needed. Nothing more could have been required of him—but to trust that God would see to it that the innkeeper used the money as the Good Samaritan intended. Chaplains understand this kind of situation. Often chaplains "hand off" the people they serve—when their assignment ends, or for other reasons. Provision for follow-up care may be required, but after suitable arrangements are made, the chaplain is left to trust God that needs will be met.

In some scenarios, only physical needs are addressed. The Good Samaritan ministered only to the man's physical needs, as far as we know. Other stories in this book involve chaplains who addressed spiritual needs, and the work of today's chaplain typically involves dealing with emotional and spiritual matters. But at times chaplains are able to help only with physical issues: finding shelter for a family made homeless by a storm, handing out water and ice, seeing that hungry people get food. There might not be time—or an open door—for spiritual ministry in any given situation. For chaplains, it's "first things first;" at times, physical and material needs are the "first things." Yet, the mere example of loving care that we offer may minister silently but powerfully to the spiritual needs of the individual.

> *I was hungry and you gave Me something to eat; I was thirsty, and you gave Me drink; … naked, and you clothed Me; I was sick, and you visited Me … to the extent that you did it to one of these brothers of Mine … you did it to Me.*
>
> Matthew 25: 35–36, 40

Chapter 2

MINISTERING TO THE ENEMY

Ananias Serving Saul

Acts 9: 1-31; 22:1-16

Ananias was one of God's disciples, a convert in the early years following Jesus' time on earth. He was ready to serve Him, so when he heard God call his name, Ananias responded immediately. "Here I am."

God had a mission for his disciple who lived in the city of Damascus, now in the nation of Syria. Ananias was to minister to a man who was in distress. He didn't have to go far to do God's bidding—just to the house of Judas[9] in Damascus. There he was to help a man who had lost his sight.

God had prepared the man for Ananias' visit. "He is praying to me," God said, "and he has seen a vision that you will lay your hands on him so that he might see again."

---

9   The Bible doesn't tell us anything about this Judas, but likely he was a believer; the house may also have been an inn or boarding house.

On the surface, it seemed like an ideal ministry opportunity for Ananias. He could be part of a dramatic event, having a role in the restoration of a man's vision. It appeared that the man was psychologically prepared for Ananias' visit after having lost his sight three days earlier. And Ananias wouldn't have to spend time and money traveling to do his work.

But there was a major catch. The man was Saul[10] of the city of Tarsus. This Saul had a reputation among God's followers, and it was far from a good one. Saul was a Christian-hater who acted on his hatred by persecuting God's saints in Jerusalem, both men and women. He broke into their houses and dragged them away. If they believed in Christ, he put them in prison; if they did not re- nounce their faith, he put them to death. Saul witnessed the murder of Stephen, encouraging those who stoned this believer. Saul's anti- Christian zeal was so intense that when Christians fled Jerusalem, Saul followed them.

Worse still, Ananias knew that Saul had come to Damascus with written authority to arrest anyone who trusted in Christ and to bring them in chains to Jerusalem. Ananias was not a Christian refugee from Jerusalem; he was a resident of Damascus. But as a Jewish convert to Christianity, Ananias would have been one of Saul's targets.

So he pushed back. "Lord, I have heard from many how this man harmed your saints in Jerusalem," he said, "and now he has

---

10   Saul was his Hebrew name, Paul his Roman (Gentile) name. The author of the Book of Acts (Luke) used the Hebrew name exclusively in the early chapters, but the use of "Paul" became predominant later in the book as Paul entered into his ministry to the Gentiles.

come to Damascus with authority from the chief priests to bind all who call on Your name." Undoubtedly Ananias was afraid of this man who was "breathing threats and murder"[11] against the Christians in Damascus.

God had a plan that would protect Ananias, however, and He shared it with his disciple. Saul had been (or soon would be) converted to Christianity.[12] "I have chosen Saul to do my work," He said. "He will take my Name to the Gentiles and the kings and sons of Israel." God also explained that Saul, who had caused great suffering for those who followed the risen Savior, would himself suffer as a believer. The chief persecutor would join the ranks of the persecuted.

Saul had been blinded by an intense, heavenly-bright light as he neared Damascus. He heard the voice of Jesus asking why Saul persecuted Him (by persecuting His followers). But Saul saw no one; he only heard the voice. It had to be a scary time for Saul and his entourage. Saul's traveling companions—left speechless by the event—could do nothing for him except bring him to Damascus as Jesus directed.

But Ananias could help, and he did. He believed God's promise regarding Saul—so much so that when he spoke to Saul at Judas' house, Ananias called him "brother." After laying hands on Saul, Ananias said to him, "The Lord Jesus, who appeared to you on the

---

11   Acts 9:1

12   Generally, the commentators believe that Saul was converted while he was still on the road to Damascus – he referred to Jesus as "Lord" after hearing His voice – though some maintain that the conversion occurred in Damascus.

road, has sent me so that you might see again, and be filled with the Holy Spirit." And he said, "Brother Saul, receive your sight."

Saul regained his vision immediately. Then Ananias told Saul that he (Saul) would be God's witness to all men of what he had seen and heard. At Ananias' direction, Saul was baptized.

Then Saul ate—he had been without food and water for three days—and the strength that had left him returned. Immediately, Saul went to the synagogue to tell others about Jesus.

Thus, through God's mercy[13] and the faithfulness of one disciple, another man became God's disciple—and in turn, a minister to those in distress.[14]

Epilogue

After his dramatic conversion, Saul spent several days with Christ's disciples in Damascus. Then, instead of continuing to hang out with other people, he went to Arabia for a long period of time, where "he was alone with God, thinking through the implications of his encounter with the risen Christ on the Damascus road."[15] After this, he returned to Damascus, and then he went to Jerusalem. There, the Jews plotted to kill him. Christ's followers helped him escape by lowering him in a large basket through an opening in the wall. He tried to connect with Christ's disciples in Jerusalem,

---

13   In 1 Timothy 1:12-13, Paul wrote that even though he had been a persecutor, he was shown mercy and put into the Lord's service.

14   The next chapter gives an example of Paul's ministry as a chaplain.

15   The Ryrie Study Bible, New American Standard Translation (Moody Press, Chicago, 1978), footnote to Galatians 1:17. Reprinted by permission of Moody Publications, Chicago IL.

but they were afraid of him because they did not believe he was one of them. Then Barnabas took hold of Saul, bringing him to the disciples and telling them of Saul's Damascus experience. The other disciples finally accepted him, and for a time Saul spoke out in public, but another threat from the Jews led to the disciples' taking him to Caesarea and then Tarsus. But Saul's conversion had evidently taken the pressure off of the Christ followers. "So the church throughout all Judea and Galilee and Samaria enjoyed peace, being built up; and, going on in the fear of the Lord and in the comfort of the Holy Spirit, it continued to increase."[16]

Thoughts for the Chaplain

Ananias was ready to go when God called. Ananias may have been busy at the time, but if he was, his response, "Here am I," meant that he was available at God's call. He had a chaplains' awareness that God could call at any moment and a sensitivity to His leading. He didn't say, "I'm busy, how about tomorrow," or "call Joseph—he has time."

The matter was urgent. "Arise and go," God said. The man was praying, ready to be ministered to. It was a teachable moment, and those moments don't last. So Ananias went—after God reassured him that he would be safe.

Ananias shared his fears with God. When he learned who he was to help, Ananias had a normal human reaction—fear. The assignment seemed to be out of Ananias' comfort zone. He might have refused to do what God asked. Or he might have taken on the task without objection, hiding his fear. But he took his concerns to the Lord.

He pushed back. Then, he accepted God's explanation and took on the mission after his fears had been dealt with.

Ananias ministered to the enemy. Saul likely had become a follower of God by the time Ananias got to the house where Saul was staying. Nevertheless, Ananias was about to lay hands on the body of a man who had laid violent hands on Ananias' brothers and sisters in Christ. Saul's zeal to rid the world of Christians led him to travel 150 miles from Jerusalem to Damascus. He was the ringleader, the chief prosecutor in the campaign against God's people. Besides fearing for his life, Ananias might also have been thinking, "a man as horrible as this could never become a Christian, so why should I risk my life?" Or, "he doesn't deserve help." Or, "let's wait a few months to make sure he really has changed." Or even, "Joseph definitely is the man for this dangerous assignment."

Following God's command ("Go and do what I say"[17]) may have been a difficult step for Ananias, but God equipped him to do it.

God prepared Saul for Ananias' visit. The overpowering bright light… hearing the voice of Jesus but not being able to see Him … the blinding that persisted for several days without Saul's knowing if and when he would see again. All things considered, God had Saul in the teachable moment we mentioned earlier. He was humbled, ready to receive God's messenger. It was a "helpable moment" for Ananias.

God was in it, so He cleared the way. Ananias only had to be obedient.

---

17   Acts 9:13 (The Living Bible, TLB)

Ananias followed through with encouraging information and exhortation. His sight restored, Saul looked up at Ananias. Ananias was ready with information and encouragement, telling Saul what had happened and what lay ahead. Then he pressed Saul with the urgency of the next step. "Why do you delay?" he asked. "Arise and be baptized, and wash away your sins, calling on His name."[18]

God called an ordinary person to do something He could have done. The God who blinded Saul could have unblinded him. But He chose to work through a human, as He often does. He just needed a godly individual who was willing to serve. Ananias was that person.

Though as a Jew he was a devout follower of the law and was well thought of by all the Jews in Damascus,[19] Ananias was not a priest or other religious big shot. Nor did he, as far as we know, have special training for ministry. He might have been intimidated by Saul's intellectual horsepower; Saul was a religious scholar trained by Gamaliel, a renowned Jewish teacher. But all Ananias had to do was what God directed him to do. He was an ordinary man called to do an extraordinary thing. Matthew Henry explained it this way:

> It does not appear that he [Ananias] was apostolically ordained. But why were not some of the apostles from Jerusalem sent for upon this great occasion, or Philip the evangelist? … [the answer is that] surely Christ would employ a variety of hands in eminent services … and thereby put honour upon the heads of those who

---

18   Acts 22:16

19   Acts 22:12

> were ... obscure, to encourage them ... and because
> he would direct us to make much of the [ministry
> opportunities] that are where our lot is cast... .[20]

Ananias served in the "workplace," outside the church, ministering to a man who was in distress. His ministry brought physical comfort and healing, spiritual care and guidance, encouragement and exhortation. He was a chaplain that day in Damascus.

God will prepare us for ministry, but it may take time, we may face opposition, and we may need the help of fellow Christians. When God confronted Saul on the Damascus road, He saw the man for what he would become. But when he was converted, Saul wasn't immediately ready to take on the major assignment God had for him. Although we don't know the curriculum, God took him to school in Arabia. Then God gave him on-the-job training when both Jews and Christians rejected him—a preview of the persecution God told Ananias that Saul would experience. A fellow believer, Barnabas, stepped in to argue Saul's case to the other disciples, a vital act that eventually led to the building up of His church throughout the land. Over time, God prepared Saul (Paul) to take His Name "to the Gentiles, and the kings and sons of Israel."

God may "take us to school" to prepare us, permit opposition to sharpen us, and require us to call on fellow Christians for help. If all this happens, don't be surprised. It happened to Saul. And he went on to be not only a great evangelist and teacher but also a chaplain as will be seen in the next chapter and chapter nine.

---

20   Matthew Henry, op. cit., Vol. VI, p. 114

I thank Christ Jesus our Lord, who has strengthened me, because He considered me faithful, putting me into service, even though I was formerly a blasphemer and a persecutor and a violent aggressor. Yet I was shown mercy because I acted ignorantly in unbelief; and the grace of our Lord was more than abundant, with the faith and love which are found in Christ Jesus.

1 Timothy 1:12-14

Chapter 3

SHIPWRECKED! — MINISTERING DURING A STORM

Chaplain Paul

Acts 27:1 through 28:15

"He was the chaplain of the ship ..."[21]

THE SHIP WAS SAILING NEAR the island of Crete, carrying some 276 souls, when the Nor'easter slammed into it. On board were a number of prisoners, one hundred guards under the command of a centurion,[22] crewmembers, the ship's master, and likely others. It was in the fall of the year, sometime around 60 A.D.

Those in charge of the ship had been hoping to reach a safe harbor on Crete's western end. Their plan was to avoid contrary winds by sailing in the shelter of the island, which lies in the northern

---

21   Matthew Henry, op. cit., Vol. VI, p. 346, writing about Paul.

22   A centurion was the equivalent of a non-commissioned officer, e.g., a sergeant.

Mediterranean Sea below what is now known as Greece and Turkey. But the storm, with typhoon-strength winds, got to them before they reached the harbor. For all practical purposes, it took control of the ship's tiller and command of its sails, pushing the ship out into the open sea.

Until that point, the sailing had been reasonably good. The men originally put to sea at Caesarea, a port city on the eastern Mediterranean, located in what is now Israel. The ultimate destination was Italy. They port-hopped along portions of the eastern and northern Mediterranean, sticking close to land for shelter from the winds as they went. Even so, they encountered strong headwinds that slowed their pace as they passed between the large island of Cyprus and what is now Turkey. They transferred at Myra (in modern Turkey) to a ship loaded with wheat and resumed their travel to Italy. But when the ship pulled into Fair Havens, a port on the south side of Crete, the leaders had reached a decision point.

Fall was not a great time to sail on the Mediterranean because of seasonal storms. One of the ship's prisoners—perhaps the most prominent among them—a Christian named Paul who had sailed the Mediterranean before, knew about the danger. He stepped forward to urge that the ship stay at Fair Havens for the winter.

Paul had been taken into custody by Roman soldiers in Jerusalem, to protect him from angry Jews who accused him of telling people to disobey Jewish laws. He was transferred to Caesarea for trial before the Roman governor and then—after Paul appealed to Caesar—was ordered sent to Rome to appear before the Roman emperor. Paul was accompanied by a man named Luke and another Christ-follower, one Aristarchus from Thessalonica.

Paul explained to the ship's leaders that continuing on with the voyage would certainly result in damage and loss, not only to the ship and its cargo, but also to human lives. The contrary argument—put forth by the pilot and captain, and bought by the centurion (who seemed to have a lot to say about the matter)—was that the Fair Havens harbor was not suitable for waiting out the winter weather. The decision-makers opted to try to reach Phoenix, a harbor that was more favorable for wintering. [23] So they set sail in an inviting, mild south wind.

Just as Paul had warned, the Nor'easter overtook the ship on its way to Phoenix. When the storm hit, the men did the best they could to survive. They under girded the ship with cables to keep it from breaking up if they ran aground, took the lifeboat on board, let the sea anchor down, and jettisoned some cargo along with the ship's tackle.

But they could not control the ship—not that day, and not for several weeks. They did not see the sun or stars during that long period, so they didn't know where they were, and they didn't know where they were headed. They needed the stars for navigation; compasses had not yet been invented. They were lost at sea.

After a while, the men began to lose hope that they would survive. They stopped eating, even though there was plenty of food on the ship.

Then Paul stepped forward a second time. After reminding the leaders that they should have followed his advice back in Fair

---

23   Luke, who wrote the Book of Acts, did not explain why the Phoenix harbor was more suitable for wintering, but it may be that ships docked in the Fair Havens harbor were more vulnerable to damage from the storms.

Havens, Paul brought a word from God. The bad news: the ship would be lost, run aground on an island. The good news: everyone would survive. An angel of the Lord had appeared to Paul, telling him not to fear, that he must stand before Caesar, and that "God will save the lives of all those sailing with you."

"I believe God," Paul told them. But some of the sailors did not. When it appeared that the ship was approaching land[24]—raising the possibility of running aground—the sailors were caught letting down the lifeboat. They pretended that they were going to lay out anchors but instead planned an escape. Once again, Paul spoke up. "You won't make it if these men leave the ship," Paul told the centurion, acknowledging that the sailors were needed if there was to be any chance of controlling the ship. So the soldiers cut the lifeboat loose, foiling the escape plan.

Then Paul urged the men to eat so that their strength might be preserved. He reassured them: "not a hair from the head of any of you will perish." Then he took bread, gave thanks to God in the presence of all, and began to eat. The men were encouraged and they, too, ate. When they had eaten enough, they began to lighten the ship by throwing the wheat into the sea.

When dawn came, they saw land—a bay and a beach—and they attempted to drive the ship onto the beach. The ship grounded on a reef, however, and began to break up. The soldiers then complicated a chaotic situation by plotting to kill the prisoners so that none could swim away and escape. The centurion quashed the plan, however, because he wanted to bring Paul through safely.

---

24   The water depth, measured by sounding, continued to decrease. This meant that land was nearby.

Some who were on the ship swam to shore, while others rode in by clinging to planks and other items from the ship. But all made it alive, just as God had promised.

"...and [the people on the ship] had reason to be proud of their chaplain ..."[25]

Epilogue

It had been an incredible story of survival through a killer storm—a nightmarish voyage of some 500 miles from Crete to an island called Malta. God not only saved them, but also guided them in the general direction of their destination. Malta lies at the western end of the Mediterranean Sea next to Sicily at the toe of the boot that is Italy. More important to the travelers' survival, however, was the fact that friendly people inhabited the island. They greeted the refugees with a fire to warm them as a cold rain fell.

Though the life-threatening voyage was over, Paul wasn't through ministering. He had plenty of time to serve others; as it turned out, the travelers stayed on the island for three months until winter passed. God showed His power to the natives right after the shipwreck survivors went ashore, when Paul shook off a viper that bit him after it came out of a bundle of sticks that Paul placed on the fire. Paul suffered no harm, much to the astonishment of the natives.

The island's leader, Publius, entertained the newcomers for three days. After Paul learned that Publius' father was ill, he prayed

---

25   Matthew Henry, op. cit., Vol. VI, p. 346

and laid hands on the sick man, and he was healed. Others on the island who had diseases came to Paul to be cured.

The people treated Paul and his companions with respect and supplied them with all their needs when they were ready to depart Malta in a ship that had wintered at the island. The ship stopped in Sicily, providing Paul and his companions an opportunity to connect with other believers and to stay with them for seven days. Then the ship sailed on to Rome, its final destination. Christ-followers came from a distance to visit with Paul and his friends. This lifted Paul's spirits, for when he saw them, "he thanked God and took courage."[26]

Thoughts for the Chaplain

In the ordinary case, the disaster relief chaplain shows up after the storm has done its damage. Here, our chaplain was in the storm. Yet this inspiring story brings lessons in the leadership and encouragement that chaplains can provide not only in the eye of the storm but also during the chaotic recovery period after the storm has passed through.[27] And it underscores the importance of an unqualified commitment to God and faith that His wisdom will control the outcome, no matter how desperate the circumstances.

Paul kept his head and used his experience to give practical advice. Disaster produces the best and worst of human behavior—good judgment and bad, selflessness and selfishness, positive action and

---

26   Acts 28:15

27   Disasters are sometimes classified as natural or manmade. Since the ship's leaders in this story chose to sail despite the possible dangerous weather, this disaster was as much manmade as natural.

paralysis or panic. Some people are obedient to authority; others refuse to follow directions such as evacuation orders. Level heads and calm leadership are badly needed. At the Fair Havens decision point, Paul advised caution based on his knowledge and experience, only to see the leaders choose the ideal over the safe and practical. Likely they rationalized, "Phoenix is just up the coast," gambling on the seductively mild south wind—and losing to the Nor'easter. When the sailors selfishly tried to leave the ship, Paul was there to point out that the sailors would be needed in the hours ahead. When the men refused to eat—likely because they were paralyzed by fear, bound by hopelessness, or too busy trying to save the ship— Paul stood up to tell them they needed food for strength. He was aware of the men's needs and was available with wise counsel.

Paul persisted even though his first advice was ignored. After the ship's leaders rejected Paul's admonition to stay at Fair Havens, Paul might have felt justified in withdrawing to his place among the prisoners, content to let the leaders deal with the consequences of their decision. After all, he was a mere prisoner—what status did he have before those in charge? And anyway, he was headed toward what he may have suspected to be a death sentence in Rome.

But Paul did not let rejection and his status on the ship stop him from continuing to interject himself into the ship's circumstances. And before long, the people began to listen to him; he became a leader on the ship. Paul took advantage of the fact that the leadership "center of gravity" can shift during crisis, depending on who has the required knowledge, initiative and persistence, and stability in crisis. Paul was not shy; after the storm hit, he reminded the ship's decision makers that he had given good advice before, even though the advice had not been taken.

Paul's calm, rational approach in the midst of chaos ultimately brought acceptance after initial rejection of his advice. Chaplains who served victims of flooding and landslides in the Seattle area in January 2009 had a similar experience. A Homeland Security Coordinator wrote:

> Initially, there was some uncertainty on the part of the Federal Emergency Management Agency (FEMA) about having chaplains work in a Disaster Recovery Center (DRC). However, over the duration of the DRC, the chaplains played a big part in comforting victims and allaying their fears. FEMA representatives brought a number of very distraught citizens directly to the chaplains' table before beginning to process them. Many of us observed firsthand that the chaplains are very gifted and compassionate in dealing with people in crisis situations. At the DRC the chaplains were able to calm, relax, and make the experience a very non-threatening and friendly place for people to visit.[28]

Today's chaplains, like Paul, can be in the eye of the storm but in the center of God's will where they are protected—and used to His glory.

---

28   From an article by Curt Beaupre, Homeland Security Coordinator, Pierce County Emergency Management, *Team Washington Homeland Security Update, Winter 2009.* Reprinted by permission of Curt Beaupre.

God spoke at the darkest hour, providing crucial knowledge to Paul in the midst of disaster. After the men had given up hope, God sent his angel to reveal to Paul that all those aboard would be saved. We know that God did not give Paul this information until the storm hit, because back in Fair Havens Paul—speaking from his own experience—had warned the men that lives would be lost. It is important to note that Paul didn't use the lack of a specific word from God as an excuse for not speaking out then. Instead, he said what made sense to him at the time in an effort to avoid disaster. Contemporary chaplains have similar experiences—we have to rely on common sense solutions initially, then see God's will clearly revealed. In some circumstances, what seems like our own practical ideas have turned out to be God-directed.

Paul took a firm stand for God and witnessed for Him before the others. Paul left no doubt: "I believe God," he said after sharing God's revelation that everyone would survive. When he broke bread, Paul gave "thanks to God in the presence of all," publicly praying to his Lord.

Paul was a selfless encourager, and his consistency paid off. Paul overcame any fear that he might have had for his own survival and selflessly reached out beyond his own circumstances. Without wavering, he encouraged the others, and they responded over time. Eventually, Scripture tells us, all were encouraged, and all ate to regain their strength.

Paul continued to serve after the worst was over. Once safely on shore in the presence of friendly natives, warmed by a fire and knowing that a seaworthy ship lay in the harbor, Paul might have relaxed while waiting for winter to pass. But he did not. He served—from the menial chore of gathering sticks for the fire to the life-saving task of healing. It seems that he was available, approachable, and generous with his time. As God often does with chaplains, He used Paul to have a positive influence on the lives of the people he ministered to on the island. It is probably not a coincidence that Paul and his people were supplied with all their needs when they departed.

The support of fellow believers is crucial. Undoubtedly Paul, Luke, and Aristarchus gathered for prayer frequently during the episode, and the other two men surely were an encouragement to Paul. Important also were those who met Paul in Rome, for when he saw them, "he thanked God and took courage." The prayers and encouragement of other believers, both during and after crisis, are crucial parts of the chaplain's support.

> *Therefore, encourage one another and build up one another...*
>
> 1 Thessalonians 5:11

Chapter 4

RISKING YOUR LIFE TO HELP A FELLOW CHRISTIAN

Epaphroditus and Paul
Philippians 2:19-30; 4:10-19

"EPAPHRODITUS IS HOME! EPAPHRODITUS IS home!" Christians in Philippi rejoiced at the news. One of their brothers had returned home safely from a long, difficult journey to Rome and back to this city in western Macedonia (now Greece). The exact route he traveled is not known. But any of the possible routes—by sea, over land, or a combination of these two—would have been challenging, to say the least.

Epaphroditus had been on a mission to deliver a gift (money) to meet the needs of Paul, who was imprisoned (under house arrest) in Rome while awaiting trial.[29] This wasn't the first time the

---

29   This imprisonment happened when Paul was taken to Rome following the shipwreck episode described in chapter 3 of this book. See Acts 28:16-31

Christ-followers in Philippi had ministered to Paul's needs. They had sent gifts to Paul at least twice while he was in Thessalonica. But Thessalonica was less than 100 miles away and accessible by land. Rome was more than 500 miles distant by the way the raven flies—and many, many more miles by any route Epaphroditus would have taken. Epaphroditus was carrying money, making the trip even riskier.

To complicate matters further, Epaphroditus got sick after he arrived in Rome—so sick that he came close to death. Exhaustion from his trip may have made him vulnerable. Or he may have worked too hard after he arrived—he and Paul were "working and battling side by side."[30] Whatever the cause of the illness, Epaphroditus had risked his life to do God's work on behalf of a brother. But God had mercy on him, and he recovered. And God's mercy extended to Paul, who wrote that he would have had "sorrow upon sorrow" if Epaphroditus had not survived.[31]

In addition to his physical illness, Epaphroditus had another problem—he became homesick, longing for his Christian family. And he was distressed because he learned that the Philippians had heard about his illness, and he knew they would worry until they saw him again.

---

and Ryrie, op. cit., footnote to Acts 28:30 and Introduction to The Letter of Paul to the Ephesians.

30   Philippians 2:25 (TLB)

31   Paul's first sorrow may have been his imprisonment, or it may have been the recent loss of a fellow believer. Matthew Henry, op. cit, Vol. VI, p. 736

Paul surely would have benefited if Epaphroditus had continued on with him; Paul referred to him as "brother and fellow worker and fellow soldier."[32] (Paul was free to preach concerning the kingdom of God and teach concerning the Lord Jesus during his imprisonment.)[33] But he sent Epaphroditus back to Philippi so that the believers there might have joy in knowing that he had recovered and returned safely. Paul also had some things to say to the Philippians. So Epaphroditus took with him a letter that said "thank you" but also contained a message that was both inspirational and instructional. It would become known as Paul's Epistle to the Philippians.

The letter showed Paul's continuing concern for the spiritual growth of the Philippian Christians. He wrote of his desire to send Timothy—who was in Rome with Paul—to Philippi. Paul's thinking was that when Timothy would later return to Rome, he might bring Paul encouraging words on the condition of the church at Philippi. Paul explained that he had no one else to send who would be genuinely concerned for the Philippians' welfare; all the others who were with him sought their own interests, not those of Christ Jesus.

Thoughts for the Chaplain

This is a story of one chaplain (Epaphroditus) sacrificing to serve another Christian who also happened to be a chaplain (Paul).[34] We

---

32   Philippians 2:25

33   Act 28:31

34   As we saw in chapter 3, Paul himself had served as a chaplain during the storm on the Mediterranean. Another example of his chaplaincy is in

can learn much about the chaplaincy from Epaphroditus' example of both sacrifice and compassion. We can also gain insight from Paul's generous and unselfish responses as to how a Christian in need might respond to the ministering of a fellow believer. But there's more: this story shows how a fellowship of believers (the Philippians) can benefit from their generous sacrifice to support a chaplain's work. In short, this story provides an example of how God works to expand what on the surface seems to be a limited chaplain mission to an adventure with broader purpose and unexpected positive consequences.

Epaphroditus' sacrifice and compassion. The heart of chaplaincy is self-sacrifice—that is, other-focus. The courageous servant of the Lord in this story came close to the ultimate sacrifice: death for the work of Christ. Undoubtedly, Epaphroditus knew of the risks involved in making the trip. But he went anyway because a brother was in need. In fact, Paul called him a "messenger and minister to my need."[35]

Epaphroditus' story brings critical questions to contemporary chaplains: How much risk should we take in going to the aid of a fellow Christian? Does the nature and severity of the need— e.g., financial (as in Paul's case), physical illness or injury, emotional stress (e.g., burnout)—make a difference in deciding how much risk to undertake? Should we take more risk to help someone we know than someone we don't know?

Chaplains quickly learn that a fundamental rule is this: don't become part of the problem. In other words, when you minister to

Chapter 9.

35   Philippians 2:25

others, don't put yourself in a situation where you need to be rescued or given medical treatment—adding to the demands on rescue and medical workers. For example, if a chaplain is serving in a hot climate, he or she must drink water frequently to avoid heat exhaustion and the need for medical attention. The obligation of a chaplain to care for himself or herself isn't limited to physical health; we have to be mentally healthy if we are to minister effectively. Then there is the benefit of partnering. Epaphroditus apparently traveled alone; today's chaplains are urged (sometimes required) to partner with another chaplain as they minister. "And one can overpower him who is alone, two can resist him …" Ecclesiastes 4:12.

How do we decide whether to go to the aid of another where there is risk? If the chaplain-in-need is in a disaster area, the authority in charge of the area or the sponsor of our deployment may have the last word. Otherwise, we can seek the counsel of experienced people, with the wise counsel of the Holy Spirit—sought through prayer—as our guide.

Besides his sacrificial attitude, Epaphroditus also showed a chaplain's compassion when he learned that the people in Philippi knew about his illness. Perhaps he would have preferred to stay with Paul; sometimes it is difficult for a chaplain to disengage from those he or she is serving. Pat often has the bittersweet experience of parting from those she has been serving in a disaster area so that she can return home from a deployment. Epaphroditus did not want the folks back home to worry, so he accepted Paul's decision to send him back to Philippi.

The gracious and unselfish attitude of Paul. The generosity of the givers (the Philippians) was matched by the grace of the recipient.

Paul wrote that he had an abundance, that he was amply supplied by the gift from the Philippians; he had, as he said, "learned to be content in whatever circumstances I am."[36] His attitude went beyond gratitude to a desire that others would benefit from participation in Paul's ministry. He did not seek the gift itself, he said, but the blessings of spiritual growth that would come to the Philippians through their sacrificial giving. Paul wanted to see the church grow, serve, and participate in the process of ministry.

Paul did not want the Philippians to worry about Epaphroditus. He sent Epaphroditus home "all the more eagerly in order that when you see him again you may rejoice and I may be less concerned about you."[37] Paul's unselfish concern for the Philippians—the only group that shared their resources with him—was evident. And his generous approach toward the Philippians went beyond the dispatching of Epaphroditus back to Philippi. With Epaphroditus gone, Paul could surely use Timothy's continuing help, but he planned to send Timothy to Philippi. That would leave Paul without the support of anyone who, in Paul's judgment, placed Christ first in their lives.

Paul was positive as well. "I trust in the Lord that I myself shall also be coming shortly,"[38] he wrote to the church that he had helped establish years earlier. We don't know whether he did get to Philippi again, although he might have.[39] He was later released

---

36   Philippians 4:11. Paul had expenses, such as rent for the quarters in which he lived while under house arrest in Rome. See Acts 28:30.

37   Philippians 2:28

38   Philippians 2:24

39   Walvoord J.F., Zuck R.B. (ed.), "The Bible Knowledge Commentary, New Testament," (Victor Books 1985), p. 657

from his imprisonment in Rome and traveled a number of places—including Macedonia—before being rearrested and eventually martyred. Regardless, Paul's optimistic attitude, based on his faith and preserved in the book of Philippians, lives on to encourage and inspire us even today. His selflessness comes through not only in the account of Epaphroditus' story but also in his words recorded in Acts: "I consider my life worth nothing to me, if only I may finish the race and complete the task the Lord Jesus has given me ... ."[40]

The bottom line: Paul maintained a chaplain's temperament even though he himself was in distress. As he was ministered to, he ministered back! Despite his circumstances, he remained a teacher and encourager, shown clearly by his letter to the Philippians. He stayed positive. He could have chastised Epaphroditus for taking the risks involved in traveling to Rome. Instead, he edified Epaphroditus for his faithful work.

The benefit to the believers in Philippi. The Philippians gave sacrificially to meet Paul's needs; Paul wrote that their offering amounted to "a fragrant aroma, an acceptable sacrifice, well-pleasing to God."[41] Paul explained that it was not the money that pleased him most, for he had plenty; it was the spirit of love and devotion that would bring the Philippians spiritual fruit[42] and a well-earned reward: "My God shall supply all your needs according to His riches in glory in Christ Jesus,"[43] Paul wrote.

---

40   Acts 20:24 (NIV). See also 2 Timothy 4:7 ("I have fought the good fight, I have finished the course, I have kept the faith.")

41   Philippians 4:18

42   Philippians 4:17 (NKJV)

43   Philippians 4:19

What God had in mind: much more than the delivery of the gift. If we just look at the words in Philippians chapter 2, it seems that Epaphroditus started out with a narrow and specific mission: deliver the money to Paul. He was also to be a messenger to Paul, bringing news from Philippi. But God's vision of Epaphroditus' mission was much broader than the money and the news reports. Epaphroditus stayed to help Paul, not only ministering to his needs but also becoming a fellow worker and fellow soldier in Paul's efforts to spread the gospel. It may be that the Philippians intended for Epaphroditus to stay for a period of time to become part of Paul's ministry. That may be why Paul made it clear that it was his decision to send Epaphroditus back home and why he assured the Philippians that Epaphroditus' service was exemplary.

But God was working on several levels. The church at Philippi was learning, growing, and benefiting through its sacrificial giving. And both Epaphroditus and Paul provide us with examples of how a chaplain should act, whether serving as a chaplain or being ministered to by another chaplain.

Chapter 5

CREATIVITY IN MINISTERING TO OTHERS

The Healing of the Paralytic
Mark 2:1-12; Matt 9:2-8; Luke 5:18-26

THE PEOPLE INSIDE THE HOUSE were startled—and for good reason! A hole had opened suddenly in the ceiling above them. Daylight appeared because the ceiling was also the roof. The people watched in shock as the opening in the tiled roof widened, with one tile being removed after another. Then, a stretcher appeared in the opening, and it was lowered into the room with four ropes, each attached to one of the stretcher's corners. On the stretcher lay a man who had been unable to walk into the room because he was paralyzed.

Four men had lowered the stretcher through the hole they made in the roof. They wanted to get the man to Jesus, who was in the room, so that He might heal their friend. And they chose a decidedly unconventional way to present the man to the Christ. They placed the stricken man right in the center of the room where Jesus sat teaching.

The men came up with this novel approach because when they arrived, the house was filled to capacity with people who had come to see Jesus. Word had spread that Jesus was in Capernaum, and people flocked to the house where He was staying—undoubtedly some came for healing, perhaps others to hear him teach, still others to satisfy their curiosity or fulfill other motives. The crowd was so great that the men could not even get near the door with the friend they carried, so they switched to Plan B.

Jesus would reward the faith of the four men. He would restore the physical health of the man who had been dropped in front of Him, after ministering to his spiritual well being, and after dealing with some detractors. Seeing the faith of the men, Jesus addressed the paralyzed man's spiritual condition, saying, "Take courage, my son, your sins are forgiven."

This bold action did not please the scribes and Pharisees—teachers of the law—who were in the room. Not having the courage to speak out loud, they thought to themselves, "This man speaks blasphemy." They had been taught that only God could forgive sins, and they were not willing to believe that Jesus was the Son of God.

Jesus read their minds. He then chose to prove his deity through an action that could be seen by all—physical healing. He said to the paralytic, "Get up, pick up your stretcher, and go home." And the man did.

The Bible tells us that all who were present were amazed and began to glorify God. And they were afraid because they had never seen anything like this before.

Thoughts for the Chaplain

The four chaplains acted creatively to help the paralyzed man when the conventional way was blocked. They had come expecting to enter the house and carry their friend directly to Jesus. When they realized that approach would not work, they had several options. They might have waited, not knowing if or when they might get their friend to this miracle-worker they had heard about. Or they might have given up and returned home—perhaps to try again another day, perhaps not.

But they persisted. They "would not let Christ go without a blessing," reminiscent of the time Jacob wrestled with the angel (God) and refused to let go until God blessed him.[44] Their persistence led to creativity; the plan to lower the man through the roof was "thinking outside the house." Just getting the man onto the roof likely required some ingenuity. They had to think quickly, making an on-the-spot decision about how to get help for their friend.

As chaplains, we may be called to serve those—like the paralyzed man in the story—who are "outside the door." That is, we may have the opportunity to help people who might be turned away from assistance under ordinary circumstances. For example, a

44   The men's persistence "bespoke both their faith and their fervency ... they were in earnest, and would not go away." Matthew Henry, op. cit., Vol. V, p. 459. For the story of Jacob wrestling with the angel, see Genesis 32:24-28.

chaplain might escort an injured person to a crowded triage area at a disaster site, or to an overflowing emergency room, but find that the person might not get the timely treatment needed. A bold approach may be appropriate—for example, locating the person who is in charge and asking for help. That would be "going to the top" as the four men literally and figuratively did when they climbed to the roof and presented the man directly to Jesus.

The four chaplains acted in faith, and faith brought results. "The walk of faith is sometimes a walk of perseverance."[45] The men believed that they could get their friend to Christ and that He would heal the man. To Jesus, the men's creative persistence in the face of obstacles illustrated their faith. So He healed the man. And here is an important point for the chaplain: the faith of the four chaplains helped start the divine healing process. Some assert that when the Scripture says "seeing *their* faith" Jesus healed the man, "their" probably refers to the four friends, i.e., the four chaplains.[46] Others believe that "their" refers to all five men. Either way, the faith of the four chaplains was crucial to the healing because the Bible says "their" faith, not "his." We see a similar example in the story of the centurion, whose faith alone led to Jesus' long-distance healing of the centurion's servant.[47]

---

45   The New Spirit Filled Bible, Thomas Nelson Inc., Nashville, TN 2002, p. 518

46   "'Their faith' refers not so much to [the paralytic], for his [condition] hindered him from the exercise of faith, but [the faith of those] that brought him." Matthew Henry, op. cit., Vol. V, p. 459.

47   See Matthew 8:5-13. "Truly I say to you, I have not found such great faith with anyone in Israel," Jesus said of the centurion. Matthew 8:10.

We should also note that the men acted not just out of faith but also from compassion and generosity in that they gave their time to help the man. They also risked being physically removed from the roof by the home's owner, or perhaps falling off the roof.

Jesus addressed the spiritual need before the physical need, by forgiving sin first. The conventional wisdom is that chaplains do it the other way around—meeting physical (and emotional) needs first, then ministering to the spiritual needs as the opportunity presents itself.

Some commentators teach that Jesus addressed the spiritual first in this episode because the physical problem had its roots in sin.[48] Others say that the point may be that Christ simply saw spiritual healing as the greater need and dealt with that need first.[49] Without getting into a theological debate, it is enough to say that the conventional wisdom may not always be the right approach in any given scenario facing a chaplain.

True, the biblical story is different from contemporary circumstances because the paralyzed man was presented directly to Jesus in the flesh while He was on earth, and Jesus decided which need to deal with first. However, as chaplains we can present the decision to Christ by praying for God's guidance regarding the order in which we should address needs.

We can expect critics. Jesus had his detractors, and today's chaplains have theirs. There are the "experts" who criticize the goals sought and methods used by chaplains; "religious" people who have rigid spiritual views that get in the way of ministering to needy

---

48   See Matthew Henry, op. cit., Vol. V, p. 459.

49   See footnotes to Matthew 9:2 and John 9:2, The Ryrie Study Bible, op. cit.

people in the circumstances in which they are found; those who say that the people we are serving are not worthy of help (maybe because they don't seem to be helping themselves); and those who question our qualifications as chaplains. There will be those who say "it can't be done" when they learn of the chaplain's plans. And some people, like the scribes and Pharisees in this chapter's story, will keep their negative thoughts to themselves, waiting for an opportunity to share their criticisms with others. Satan attacks in many different ways!

Jesus silenced his detractors by performing a miracle—the man stood up and walked. He did not argue with the cynics or even attempt to reason with them. He just went about doing what He knew needed to be done, setting a great example for today's chaplains.

Of course, we don't have the power to perform miracles ourselves. But we can get in touch with the One who can. A prayer asking for a miracle may be appropriate; a quick prayer for guidance is always proper. As Christian chaplains, we have an advantage in that we have a supernatural resource available to us as we pray in faith.

In some cases, a dialogue with the adversary may bring about a change of heart. A confrontation may be called for, but the old saying, "don't argue with a fool," may also apply.

The chaplain's work can bring glory to God in the eyes of many people. Pharisees and teachers of the law from every village of Galilee and Judea and from Jerusalem came to listen to Jesus on that day of healing. They came, perhaps, without the best of motives. But they went home glorifying God because they had never seen anything like this—only God could have done it. And so it can be with the work of chaplains, doing God's will in the public square for all to see, showing that God still meets people's needs two millennia after Jesus healed the paralyzed man's body and soul.

And the power of the Lord was present for Him to perform healing.

Luke 5:17

Chapter 6

"WHAT SHALL I DO?" WHAT A LITTLE JAR OF OIL AND A LOT OF FAITH CAN DO

Elisha and the Widow
2 Kings 4:1-7

DRIP, DRIP, DRIP. THE LAST drops of oil trickled from the jar, and then it was empty. But this is a story of abundance, not emptiness, through the intervention of a godly man who ministered to a woman in great need.

THE WOMAN WAS DESPERATE. SHE had been handed a double dose of disaster. First, her husband died. Then a creditor came, threatening to take her two sons as slaves in payment for money her husband had owed.

Her husband had been a "son of the prophets," likely an apprentice or student of those who proclaimed God's message to the people and their leaders. He was a godly man—feared the Lord, his widow said—but he left a debt. And the creditor chose to follow the secular custom of the day by taking the sons as slaves instead of heeding the words of Moses by allowing the sons to work off the debt as hired men.[50]

So the woman cried out to Elisha—a man of God—for help. As one of the prophets, he knew her late husband, for she referred to the husband as "your servant." And Elisha, who had been a student himself—under the prophet Elijah—came to her.

"What shall I do?" he asked. Then he followed up with a question: "What do you have in your house?" He wanted to know what she had that she might use to raise cash. But she had to admit that she had nothing—except for a single jar of oil. She had sold everything else to keep her sons from slavery, but it wasn't enough.

Elisha had a plan, one that required her to be part of the solution. First, he told her to borrow empty pots and pans from all of her neighbors. She was to get many, rather than few, of the empty vessels. Second, she and her sons were to go into their house, shut the door, and start pouring oil from the jar into the pots and pans, setting them aside when they were full.

She did as Elisha directed. The sons brought the pots and pans to her, and she poured... and poured ... and poured! There came a moment, though, when her request for another empty vessel brought a response, "every vessel is full," from her son. And the oil stopped flowing from the jar.

---

50   Leviticus 25:39-41

Then she told Elisha about the amazing thing that had happened. He said, "Go sell the oil and pay your debt." There was more than enough oil for that purpose, so Elisha added, "you and your sons can live on the rest."

Thoughts for the Chaplain

Elisha gave the woman responsibility. He opened with, "what shall I do?" He might have reached for his wallet and asked his fellow prophets to do the same, or he might have canvassed the neighborhood asking for donations of cash. But as quickly as he raised the question of what he might do, he turned the question to what she might do. And he had some thoughts on the subject! For Elisha, "What shall I do?" was a rhetorical question because God had given him a plan. The first step in the plan concerned what the widow could do. So without waiting for her to answer his question, he told her what to do.

As chaplains, we might be able to approach a person in distress as did Elisha. That is, it may turn out that person we are ministering to can be part of the solution. Obviously, some persons may be physically or mentally incapable of participating. But their involvement, where it is possible, can build self esteem and help the person return to normal living.

Sometimes the individual's contribution may come later, and it may be in the form of "passing on the blessing" to another. For example, one of our chaplains tells of a man in his sixties who watched as a crew gave his house a new roof that was needed because of damage by Hurricane Ike in 2008. The man was not able to help at that time, but when the chaplain returned to the area eight months later, the man jumped in to help with the repair of another house. Our chaplain and his colleagues were amazed to learn that the man was a master carpenter, and he contributed much to the rebuilding of the interior of one of the houses.

Discussion may help define the problem. When we come upon a person in trouble, we may know instantly what to do about the person's need. We can tell simply by looking at the situation—or, as in the Elisha's case, God may have told us what to do. But in other cases, we might begin with a dialogue that could include asking permission to assist. The conversation can help define both the problem and the solution. We may think that the person wants us to do something to meet a physical or material need, but instead what the person really wants is prayer or conversation—or both. So the upfront discussion is essential. The dialogue with the person in need can also help identify the resources that are available.

Use available resources no matter how limited. Often what's available does not seem like enough—at least from a human perspective. Surely the woman in the story thought that the one jar of oil would not satisfy her family's requirements. But in circumstances such as this one, God may be asking, "what can you do with what you have?" The chaplain may be thinking, "I have so little energy left, and there is so much more to be done," or "I need to pray for this person, but I have only a few words to say." God may be asking us to step out with what energy and what words we can give, to "teach us to make the best of what we have."[51] He may provide the rest. We (the authors) have had this experience in the financial area. For

---

51   E.g., the widow's jar of oil, see Matthew Henry, op. cit., Vol. II, p. 725

example, we have used our limited financial resources to support our chaplain ministries, and God has provided additional support from unexpected sources.

The experience of a chaplain who was involved in Hurricane Ike relief shows how God can make much out of little. He was in charge of a group of chaplains who ministered to first responders. The chaplains were asked to take over food preparation for the emergency workers to help maintain their strength and morale (the chaplain's job description often includes "additional duties as assigned"!). The city then cut the food budget in half; the chaplains (with God's help) were able to keep the food flowing. Then the budget was cut in half again. As they talked about what to do, someone reminded the group of the occasion in which Jesus multiplied the loaves and fishes. Everyone laughed ... except God.

Within an hour, a man called to say that he had a large freezer full of food that would spoil because he had no electricity. Did they want it? They did. Soon a truck arrived with the food. And the first things off of the truck? Boxes of fish fillets and loaves of bread!

Elisha got others involved. He made sure that the neighbors participated by telling the woman to borrow pots and pans from them. No doubt some of the neighbors, knowing of the woman's plight, had wanted to help her but didn't know how, so they would have been ready to respond when the woman asked. Perhaps they did not have money to give to the woman, but they were able to help in another way that might have brought them more satisfaction than giving money. In the same manner, chaplains can in appropriate circumstances suggest to the people they are serving that they should get others involved in solving the problem.

Elisha gave precise directions—but did not hover over the woman. He told the woman exactly what to do, down to directing her to close the door (maybe to keep the creditor out!). She may not have been thinking clearly because of her distress; if so, she would have appreciated specific directions. Once he gave the instructions, however, Elisha didn't micromanage. He trusted that the woman would do as told, and he trusted God that the plan would work.

Both Elisha and the woman acted with faith in supernatural intervention without voicing doubts. Elisha presented the plan to the woman without hesitating, believing that God would give the woman enough oil to solve her problem. As a man of God, he was—we surmise— "prayed up" when he came to see the widow. He was close to God, so when God revealed His plan, Elisha had confidence in what God would do.

As for the widow, when Elisha told her what to do, she didn't question whether the empty pots and pans could be filled from a single jar. She didn't respond like Jesus' disciples, who questioned whether there were enough loaves and fishes to serve the multitude that had gathered to hear Jesus speak.[52] Rewarding the faith of Elisha and the widow, God turned a little into an abundance.

Elisha's vision went beyond the woman's immediate need. "Do not get just a few pots and pans," he told her. Elisha knew that God would provide an abundance if he and the woman planned for it. And it happened—when the oil stopped flowing, the woman and

---

52   And the disciples said to Him, "Where would we get so many loaves in a desolate place to satisfy such a great multitude?" Matthew 15:33.

her sons had not only filled enough pots and pans to pay the debt, but they also had enough left over for them to live on. God supplied exactly the amount of oil needed to fill all the pots—and to meet the woman's needs!

> *Now to Him who is able to do far more abundantly beyond all that we ask or think, according to the power that works within us...*
>
> Ephesians 3:20

Chapter 7

SERVING OTHERS IN A NATURAL DISASTER

Elijah and the Widow of Zarephath

1 Kings Chapter 17

Part 1 – The Drought

IT WAS A DOOZY OF a disaster—a Category V drought, if there is such a thing, so dry that there was not even any dew to give the plants a little moisture in the early morning. Rain had not fallen in Israel for months, and the fields had turned to dust. There was no water to grow crops, no crops to produce grain, no grain to make flour, and no flour to make bread—the foundation of the Israelites' diet.

The drought spilled over Israel's northern border, rolling all the way up to the town of Zarephath on the Mediterranean Sea between Tyre and Sidon. (Zarephath was in today's Lebanon, located between Beirut and the border of Israel). The famine was about to claim the lives of two people in that small town—a widow, who was about to use her last flour and the little bit of oil she had left to prepare a meal, and her son. Despondent, without hope, she would then await what she thought was the inevitable—death by starvation for the two of them.

As she was gathering sticks for a fire to bake the bread, a man approached and asked for a drink of water. Though water was in short supply, she turned to get the water for him. But then he added a request that stopped her: "please bring me a piece of bread." Obviously, she thought, the man was unaware of the nearly empty cupboard at her house. Quickly she explained the situation to him: she was not only out of bread but also had only enough flour to bake bread for herself and her son.

The man did not withdraw his request but instead assured her that things would work out. "Don't be afraid," he said, "go ahead and make a little bread cake first and bring it to me ... then make one for you and your son." No doubt the woman wondered how she could do this, with only enough bread for two. But then the man added what, to her, must have been a most astonishing statement: "The bowl of flour will not be used up, and the jar of oil will not be empty, until the day the Lord sends rain to the land."

The man spoke with authority. He was Elijah, a prophet who God had sent to Ahab, king of Israel, to deliver news that God's judgment for Israel's sins would come down in the form of drought and famine. Ahab and his wife Jezebel did not react well to the news—in fact, they were inclined to kill the messenger. Ahab searched not only in Israel; he set off an international manhunt for Elijah.[53] God protected Elijah, though, sending him to a hiding

---

53   1 Kings 18:10

place in a remote area east of the Jordan River, where ravens fed him meat. He stayed there until the brook that had supplied his water dried up. Then God directed him back across the Jordan, and all the way to Zarephath—a journey of roughly 100 miles, most of it through Israel, where he was at the top of Ahab's "most wanted" list. There, God told Elijah, a woman would provide for his needs; he was to dwell in her household.

The woman did what Elijah told her to do. The bowl continued to supply flour, and oil flowed from the jar—just as the Lord had told her through Elijah. The widow and her household ate for many days.

Part 2—A Death in the Family

ELIJAH STAYED IN THE WOMAN'S house for a long time—perhaps two years—as part of God's plan to protect him. There was plenty of food, thanks to the bottomless bowl and jar, and all was well. Then disaster came again. The widow's son became sick and died, and immediately she turned on Elijah. "O man of God," she said, "what have you done to me? Have you come here to punish me for my sins by killing my son?"

"Give him to me," Elijah said. He took the boy to an upper room and put him on the bed, where he expressed his frustration. "O Lord my God," Elijah cried, "why have you killed the son of this widow with whom I am staying?" But then he prayed—three times—asking that the boy's life be restored. And God heard Elijah's prayer; the child came back to life, and Elijah returned him to his mother. Grateful, she said, "Now I know for sure that you are a prophet and that whatever you say is from the Lord."

Epilogue

After a time, God sent Elijah to confront Ahab, where he arranged a showdown between the true God and Baal (Ahab's god). There, God displayed his power to burn up a sacrifice after the Baal priests (who believed that Baal regulated the rain) made futile calls to their god to do the same. And then the rain returned to Israel.[54]

Thoughts for the Chaplain

We can be called to do chaplain duties even if it is not our major occupation. Elijah's main job was not as a chaplain. He was a prophet of God (some say he was the most eminent among the prophets), and he had a huge assignment from Him. God chose Elijah to bring word of His judgment to Israel when the nation had turned away from the one true God, with many worshipping Baal. To back up Elijah's prophecy, God gave him the power both to pray in the drought and to pray down the rain to lift the drought three and a half years later.

But God called Elijah to be a chaplain as well, not for all of Israel but for just one family in another land—to provide food for them, and to be there to pray for the restoration of the son's life. Though thousands may be affected by a disaster, God typically calls on chaplains to minister only to a few at any one time. The rescue of just one person or the healing of another is important to God.

---

54   1 Kings Chapter 18

God takes care of the chaplain, just as He takes care of those whom the chaplain serves. Elijah ministered to the widow and her son. But she ministered to Elijah—by giving him the first bread she made, then by inviting him to stay at her house and share meals with her family. As chaplains, we are urged not to be a part of the problem by placing an excessive burden on others. Elijah was needy—he needed a safe hiding place as well as food and lodging. But in this case, Elijah was able to serve the widow and her son, while at the same time having his needs met. God's desire was to take care of His prophet, but His prophet also took care of others. For all this to happen, Elijah needed only to be obedient to God's command to travel to Zarephath.

The prayers of ordinary people can bring powerful results. Elijah's prayers brought the child back to life. His prayers started and ended the drought. We can say, "Sure, his prayers brought miraculous results; he was a prophet anointed by God." But James wrote that Elijah was just like us—"a man with a nature like ours."[55] He had to pray three times before the child breathed again. The ordinary Christian can meet James' requirements for effective prayer—that it be fervent, earnest, preceded by confession, and offered in faith.[56]

We may be called to minister outside our comfort zone. Elijah was an Israelite. God could have sent him to any of a number of widows in Israel—in fact, Jesus said so in his "a prophet is without honor in his own country" message.[57] Instead, He sent Elijah to a woman in a

---

55   James 5:17

56   James 5:13-17

57   "There were many widows in Israel in the days of Elijah ... and yet Elijah was sent to none of them, but only to Zarephath." (Luke 4:24-6).

land of Gentiles, who were considered unclean by the Israelites. Yet Elijah stayed and was blessed with the opportunity to serve others.

The people we help can turn on us in emotional times. The widow surely was grateful to Elijah—she and her son had survived the effects of the drought and were well fed. But then when the son died unexpectedly, she immediately attacked Elijah, asking why he came to her house in the first place, her emotions overriding her memory of what Elijah had done for her. Although she attributed the boy's death to her own sins, she also blamed Elijah for punishing her for those sins merely by his presence. It took another miracle—the resurrection of her son—for her to get the right perspective on Elijah.

Our actions can be a witness to those we serve and help to increase their faith. The widow knew from her first encounter with Elijah that he was a man of God. But after God brought her son back to life, she really knew that what he said was from the Lord. And thus her faith in God grew. She showed faith at the first encounter with Elijah when she made the cake for the prophet and then was rewarded with an abundance of food. But her faith developed further as Elijah ministered to her and her son.

Elijah's reaction to the widow's attack on him when her son died undoubtedly was a key factor in the evolution of the woman's faith. Elisha could have backed away in response to the woman's outburst. Instead, he said, "Give your son to me." He did express his frustration—to God, in private—but then prayed the prayers that brought the boy back to life.

Faith is essential for the chaplain. This story is often told as an illustration of the widow's faith. But it is also a story of Elijah's faith.

Despite the danger, he traveled through Ahab's Israel to Zarephath, which was in Jezebel's homeland, when God told him to do so. When he told the widow to prepare the bread, he believed that God would provide food. And he acted in faith when he persisted in prayer to bring the son back to life, praying past his human frustration with God to ask for supernatural intervention. In fact, Elijah is in the book of Hebrews' "hall of faith" as one of the unnamed prophets whose faith led to women receiving their children back from the dead by resurrection.[58]

Chaplains must stay firm in their faith during times of persecution and national distress. The threat to Elijah's life by Ahab was very personal, but—according to divine plan—his prophecy and ministry took place during a period of turmoil and distress in Israel. The nation was in spiritual freefall, with the forces of Satan (in the form of the false god Baal) seeming to have the upper hand. God's prophets were persecuted; they were on the run, hiding in caves. Many who claimed to be people of God were unwilling to take a stand for Him. Then came the drought and famine that paralyzed the nation. But Elijah stayed true to his God and did what He asked of him.

Modern day chaplains may work in times of natural disaster such as hurricanes, tornadoes, floods, and wild fires; in terrorist attacks or mass shootings; or in economic turmoil. Spiritual warfare is a constant for these chaplains—and for Christian chaplains in all settings! For example, there may be undercurrents of religious discrimination that place barriers around the chaplain's work. "Christians" who have turned away from Truth may deny us. There may even be instances where the chaplain's life is in danger,

58   Hebrews 11:32-35

as Elijah's was. God merely asks, in those times, that we remain true to Him—living out our faith in the unseen when we face real world challenges.

> *The LORD himself goes before you and will be with you; he will never leave you nor forsake you. Do not be afraid; do not be discouraged.*
>
> Deuteronomy 31:8

Chapter 8

MINISTERING TO A PEOPLE AT WAR

Moses and the Battle with the Amalekites
Exodus 17:8-16

The Run-up to the War

THE PEOPLE OF ISRAEL THOUGHT they were safe. They had not been attacked as they traveled through the desert wilderness after God delivered them from the Egyptian Pharaoh several months earlier. Their ultimate destination was the land of Canaan—the Promised Land—but their itinerary included a visit to Mount Sinai with several intermediate rest stops on the way to that mountain. One such spot was Rephidim, a place that is not on modern maps but that is thought to have been located at the bottom of the Sinai Peninsula, across the Red Sea from Saudi Arabia. It is an area that is hilly, rocky and—being desert land—dry, with little vegetation.

But just as the travelers began to settle in for their stay at Rephidim, they were attacked without warning. The aggressors were the Amalekites, a fierce, nomadic tribe that roamed the Sinai desert to protect what they believed to be their territory, robbing and killing for pleasure. That, in itself, was bad news, but the Amalekites had an additional incentive to wage a "take no prisoners" war on Israel. They had something personal against Israel. They had descended from Amalek, grandson of Esau. The people who were gathering at Rephidim were descendants of Esau's brother, Jacob, who had taken Esau's birthright and blessing.

Esau's descendants had not forgotten what Jacob did to their patriarch. They not only wanted to keep Israel out of their territory and out of the Promised Land; they also wanted to destroy Israel.[59] To say that they did not fear God[60] was both to explain their desire to annihilate His people and to understate the ferocity that fueled them as they attacked.

The Amalekites came upon the people of Israel from the rear and—true to their brutal character—killed the weak and weary who were straggling into the camp at Rephidim.[61] On the human level, Israel was not prepared to fight against a formidable enemy. They had no military experience; this was their first battle since Moses led them out of captivity. They had no standing army and no designated military leader.

Besides, the nation was not in the kind of mood needed to sustain a battle that would test their unity and their faith in their

---

59   Psalm 83:4,7

60   Deuteronomy 25:18

61   *Ibid.*

human and divine leaders. They had just quarreled with Moses because they found no water when they arrived at Rephidim. They grumbled about his leadership. They doubted God. Only when Moses struck a rock with the staff of God did the Israelites get water.[62] And only divine intervention would save them now.

Despite the people's rotten attitude, when the Amalekites showed up, Moses immediately set about planning to defend against the attack—and the people responded to his leadership. First, he drafted Joshua as the military leader, directing him to prepare for battle by choosing men to fight for the people. Then he encouraged Joshua by telling him that he (Moses) would be stationed at the top of a hill, above the battlefield but visible to the troops, where he would be holding the staff of God. Joshua and the soldiers would be inspired, for they knew what the staff of God meant: it was a symbol of God's presence and power that had freed them from the rule of the Pharaoh and, more recently, brought water from the rock.

The Battle

So Joshua selected his soldiers, and the battle was on. Moses climbed the hill, along with Aaron (Moses' brother) and Hur (thought to be Moses' brother-in-law, husband of Moses' sister Miriam). Then a curious thing happened. As long as Moses held the staff high, Israel had the advantage. But when he dropped his hands, the Amalekites rallied. After a time, Moses became exhausted and could no longer hold the staff high. Israel's outlook was bleak. But Aaron and Hur stepped up—they found a stone for

---

62   Moses named the place where they got water Massah ("test") and Meribah ("quarrel"). Exodus 17:7

Moses to sit on, and then one stood on each side of Moses and held up his hands.

Moses' hands remained steady until sunset, and Israel's army overwhelmed the Amalekites—"mowed down and disabled" them.[63] And the battle was won.

Epilogue

With victory won, the Lord said to Moses: "Write this down: 'I will erase the memory of Amalek from under heaven.'" Moses built an altar, naming it "The Lord is My Banner," to let future generations know what God had done for His people and that He was with them. "The Amalekites have raised their fist against the Lord's throne," Moses said, "so now the Lord will be at war with Amalek generation after generation." The Amalekites would continue to pester Israel even after God's people were established in Canaan. But Saul and David both defeated them, and ultimately the Amalekites were dispersed and disappeared as a people following a final defeat during the reign of King Hezekiah. The nation of Amalek, not the nation of Israel, had been wiped out.

Thoughts for the Chaplain

Moses was a civilian leader, but he took on the role of chaplain, ministering to a nation in need and its soldiers in particular. Typically, individual chaplains serve much smaller numbers of people, but here an army was in danger, and an entire nation's fate turned on the outcome of the battle. Chaplains minister in the

---

63   Exodus 17:13 (Amplified Bible)

workplace; Moses' workplace was a battlefield where he ministered through his presence and through prayer and encouragement.

The enemy can be ferocious and intimidating and attack without warning; the challenge is to keep calm and move ahead to respond to the need. The assaults on chaplains and those they minister to often come without warning. The attacks are from those who do not play by the rules of decency and respect. As a result, the situation can appear to be overwhelming—particularly if it is a first-time experience for the chaplain, as in the case of the people of Israel who had not been attacked before.

The aggression may appear to be coming from humans, but the real enemy is Satan, who is out for our destruction just as the Amalekites wanted to destroy Israel. When confronted with what appeared to be an impossible situation, Moses didn't panic. With God's help, he developed a plan and put it into effect.

Our battles against the enemy will have ups and downs, but God will help us prevail against even the most formidable enemy. The position of Israel's army ebbed and flowed during the battle as first one side and then the other gained the advantage. In the same way, chaplains and those they serve will see highs and lows as they minister. Moses persisted even when the situation was grim; so must we. God not only helped Israel win the battle at Rephidim against an overwhelming force committed to Israel's destruction, God also helped Israel prevail ultimately in the ongoing conflict with the Amalekites—eventually destroying the people who had set out to wipe Israel from the face of the earth. We can be comforted in knowing that God not only will give victory in the skirmishes we experience as we minister but also ultimate victory over Satan.

We may be called to help people who are a pain in the neck. Moses was challenged to rescue a people who had been quarreling with him, and he responded by leading them out of peril. The people had been grumbling and complaining, raising doubts about Moses' leadership abilities. Moses could have said, "Let the Amalekites whip you; you deserve it." Yet when crunch time came, Moses stood up, ready to do what he could to save the ungrateful people. Similarly, we may be in a position to minister to people we would rather avoid; they may be negative, depressed, or unappreciative. The challenge is to focus on God's call to us in the situation, putting the negatives aside—and raising God's staff (prayer) even in the presence of detractors.

There are times when we just need to be visible to the people we are helping—the "ministry of presence." Moses could have stayed back at his headquarters, out of sight and unexposed to the battle. But he encouraged people by being there above the battlefield where the army could see him. He raised the staff of God that—like the flag a military unit carries into battle—inspired the soldiers to push on because it reminded the soldiers of the liberation from the Pharaoh and the destruction of Pharaoh's army after God parted the sea for Israel's escape.

The chaplain's ministry of presence may not be as spectacular or involve as many people as did Moses' ministry that day on the Sinai Peninsula. It may be with one person or family. But the point is the value of just being there at a time when there are no words to say or actions to take.

We will get tired, so we will need to plan for support. What Moses did was hard work, just as today's chaplains' work is often exhausting.

But Moses planned ahead by taking Aaron and Hur with him. As it turned out, their support was crucial. There is often success where members of a team work in unity to support one another.

The glory goes to God. When the battle was over, Moses gave credit to God, who had saved Moses and his people from what appeared to be certain destruction. And it was no fleeting or passing acknowledgement. He built an altar, a monument for posterity (probably of stone; there were plenty in the area). He called it "The Lord is My Banner," recognizing the importance of the visible presence of the staff of God during the battle. And he wrote down the words as God had commanded, for a reminder to current and future generations that He would go to war against those who attack His people. When we experience God's intervention that allows us to do good things, we can let people know that it is God who assures the victory. This can inspire us and others—believers and unbelievers—who are part of the shared experience.

Chapter 9

SAVING A SUICIDAL MAN IN AN EARTHQUAKE

Paul, Silas, and the Philippian Jailer
Acts 16: 16-40

THE SWORD WAS DRAWN, POISED and ready to do its deadly work. But the man who held the weapon did not intend to use it to attack another. Instead, he planned to plunge it into his own body—to end his life because he thought that if he did not do so, his superiors would. Though it was a terrible choice, he preferred to die quickly by his own hand rather than endure the torture and slow death he expected from those who had given him a task of great consequence that he thought he had failed to accomplish.

The man was a jailer in a city called Philippi, and his assignment was to assure that two prisoners who had been handed over to him by the city's magistrates[64] did not escape. He thought he was doing his job well—he put the men in the inner prison, the maximum-

---

64   Two magistrates ruled the city, a Roman colony.

security section, and for good measure put them in stocks.[65] The jail-keeper could relax, he thought, so he went to sleep.

But during the night an earthquake struck the area—a tremor powerful enough to shake the foundations of the prison, opening the prison doors and even loosening the prisoners' restraints. Awakening to realize that the prison doors were open, the jailer thought that the prisoners—including the two who had been given special attention from the authorities—had escaped. Having been warned that his life depended on keeping these two men in prison, the guard prepared to commit suicide.

The two priority prisoners were Paul and Silas; the jailer was a man who has been known through the centuries only as "the Philippian Jailer." Paul and Silas had been arrested, beaten, and jailed—ostensibly because they were teaching things that were contrary to Roman laws. But what actually led to the imprisonment was the fact that they had taken a source of income away from some local entrepreneurs. These enterprising businessmen owned a slave girl who, because she was demon-possessed, was able to tell fortunes—for a price.

Following after Paul and his colleagues,[66] the girl proclaimed that these men were "bond-servants of the Most High God, who

---

65   Stocks were a means of immobilizing a prisoner. They consisted of two boards joined together, with holes (half in each of the boards) large enough for the prisoner's wrists or ankles. Sometimes both the wrists and ankles were placed in the stocks.

66   Luke, who wrote the book of Acts, and Timothy came to Philippi with Paul and Silas but left at some point prior to Paul's departure; they were not arrested.

are proclaiming to you the way of salvation." Though this was true, Paul could not have the gospel of Christ associated with the evil represented by demons, so he commanded the demon to leave the girl. The demon departed, and the girl no longer had fortune-telling powers. That's when her masters brought Paul and Silas before the chief magistrates.

Paul and Silas had come to Philippi to preach the gospel of Jesus Christ. Truth is, they might not have gone to Philippi when they did, had they had their own way. They wanted to take their preaching mission to Asia but had been forbidden by the Holy Spirit to speak there. Then, intending to go to Bithynia,[67] they were rebuffed again because the Spirit of Jesus did not permit them. Then a vision appeared to Paul in the night, calling him to Macedonia (now known as Greece, and where Philippi was located). It was to be their first trip to what is now known as the continent of Europe.

Philippi was a Roman colony that had very few Jews—so few, in fact, that they were not able to establish a synagogue. The Romans did allow the Jews to gather to worship in Philippi but not to proselytize (the Romans thought that the Christians were a Jewish sect, so the "no proselytizing" rule applied to the Christians as well). Paul and his traveling companions were on their way to pray with the few believers in Philippi when they had their first encounter with the slave girl. It was after she persisted for many days in her demonic identification of the men of God that Paul called out the demon.

---

67   Bithynia was a region near the Black Sea in what is now Turkey.

So he and Silas ended up in prison. Though they had been beaten severely—and undoubtedly were exhausted, cold, and hungry—the two were praying and singing hymns of praise as midnight arrived. And the other prisoners were listening to them.

Then the quake came. It was dark in the prison cells, but the jailer could see that the prison gates were open, and he assumed that the prisoners had escaped. That's when he drew his sword.

"Do yourself no harm," Paul called out immediately. "We are all here!"

The guard put away his sword, approached the two men of God, and in a trembling voice said, "What must I do to be saved?"

They replied, "Believe in the Lord Jesus Christ." And they taught the word of God to the jailer and those in his household, and all were saved and baptized. The prison guard had brought Paul and Silas to his house, where he bathed their wounds and fed them. And the guard "rejoiced greatly."[68]

There is a little more to the story. After the quake, the chief magistrates sent word that Paul and Silas were to be released. This did not satisfy Paul, who returned to the prison along with Silas. "They have beaten us in public without trial, men who are Romans, and have thrown us into jail," Paul said, "and now they are sending us away secretly? No, let the magistrates themselves come and release us." On learning that the men were Romans, the magistrates were afraid. But they went to the prison and brought the men out, begging them to leave the city.

---

68   Acts 16:34

Paul and Silas then went to the house of Lydia, whom they had led to the Lord upon their arrival in Philippi. There, they encouraged the brethren and then left Philippi.

At midnight I shall rise to give thanks to You because of Your righteous ordinances.

Psalm 119:62

Thoughts for the Chaplain

Partnership can be a key to effective chaplaincy. This story is about two chaplains—suffering, ministering, and rejoicing together. Although Paul is the better known of the two, Silas was a versatile man who contributed much to the advancement of the gospel in general and Paul's ministry in particular. He traveled with Paul, he was a leader in the Jerusalem church, and he wrote for both Paul and Peter under the name "Silvanus." No doubt Paul and Silas encouraged and supported one another during their persecution at Philippi.

Chaplains may be called on to minister to those who persecute them, and the chaplains may put themselves in jeopardy by doing so. When the earthquake freed them, Paul and Silas might have refused to help the person who had put them in the most uncomfortable conditions possible. No doubt they realized that they might remain imprisoned if the guard survived. They could have let the jailer kill himself and then walked away as free men. But they acted to stop the man from plunging the sword into his own body. They did what was needed to stop a suicidal man from carrying out his intentions. That is, Paul responded quickly after becoming aware of the jailer's plan, and he needed only a few words ("We are all here") to let the jailer know that his suicidal motivation was without foundation.

Prayer and praise in the midst of adversity pays off. Despite their stark circumstances, Paul and Silas prayed and praised God during the evening hours. And they did so openly—so that other prisoners, and no doubt the jailer, could hear. So when the prison doors flew open and Paul helped the jailer spare his own physical life, the jailer knew that he had to attend to his spiritual life. He knew this because of Paul and Silas' bold witness in the prison, and perhaps also because he had heard of the slave girl's pronouncements. So he came trembling to Paul and Silas, asking what he must do to be saved. The pay-off for Paul and Silas was not only in the conversion of the jailer, but also the conversion of his family members—and possibly of other prisoners. The two were with the jailer and his family as they rejoiced over their salvation. And their physical needs—treatment of their wounds and food—were met.

Like Paul and Silas, today's chaplains may get exhausted and hungry but are called on to pray and witness for God nevertheless.

Strike while the iron is hot. When the jailer came with his question, Paul and Silas might have said, "We'll deal with this later—right now we need to get out of here, get something to eat, get our wounds bandaged, and get some rest." But this was a teachable moment for the jailer, and Paul and Silas not only told him how to be saved but also "spoke the word of the Lord" to him and his family.

Contemporary chaplains have similar "teachable moment" opportunities. A simple question, "How are you holding up after [the hurricane, tornado, flood, death of a loved one, loss of your job]?" can open the way to discussion of the individual's or family's spiritual needs. In one case, the survivor of a hurricane responded to the question by revealing that she had lost her house and all her possessions and that her church was no longer functioning. The chaplain was able to minister to her spiritual need and help her get established in a local church whose doors were still open. Another hurricane survivor responded by reporting that he had lost his job and could not provide for his family. As in the story of the jailer, the chaplain led this man into a relationship with the Lord. Because of their circumstances, these survivors were ready to listen.

Standing up for God can get us in trouble. When he heard the slave girl tell everyone why Paul and Silas were in Philippi, Paul was not going to allow Satan (through his demon) to corrupt the gospel by association. Paul's exorcising the demon got him and Silas into trouble—mainly because his action cost lots of money for the slave girl's masters. We should be prepared for the possibility that what we do might bring opposition from someone whose financial interests are harmed by our activities. When confronting Satan, we may also experience a backlash from those through whom Satan is attempting to work.

Chaplains act to protect their fellow believers. It is not easy to understand why Paul insisted that they return to the prison and be released by the magistrates. But consider these possibilities. Having the magistrates openly involved in the release of the men made it clear to all that Paul and Silas, as Roman citizens, should have been given a fair trial and should not have been beaten. And it may have signaled to the majority Roman population of Philippi that they needed to go easy on the Christians.

But there may be an even larger point: Paul and Silas might have been released the day before the earthquake, had they brought up their Roman citizenship when they were taken into custody. So this means that the earthquake likely was about the salvation of the Philippian jailer and his family, and perhaps other prisoners—not about the release of Paul and Silas! God will find a way—sometimes dramatic, like an earthquake—to see that His salvation message is heard.

God may open and close options for us in our ministry—with consequences for us. Paul and his traveling companions wanted to serve in Asia; the Holy Spirit said "no." They wanted to carry the message to Bithynia, but the Spirit of Jesus said "no." Perhaps they would not have been harmed had they gone to those places. But God did give a green light: He sent them to a city where they would suffer and be tested—and where their witness while suffering would lead others to Jesus Christ. Like Paul and Silas, we are asked to listen to the wise and discerning Spirit of God as we plan our work.

And His song will be with me in the night, a prayer to the God of my life.

Psalm 42:8

Chapter 10

PROTECTING DAVID: A DRAMA IN FOUR ACTS, WITH AN EPILOGUE

Featuring the Chaplain Relay Team
1 Samuel chapters 19-21

THIS IS THE STORY OF a series of chaplains who ministered to a man in distress who was running from a man who had murderous plans. The story opens with the order to kill the fleeing man.

Act 1 (1 Samuel 19)
Scene 1 (19:1-3)

"Put David to death," Israel's King Saul said to his son and his servants. But the son, Jonathan, was not willing to follow his father's orders because David was his best friend. So Jonathan went to David and warned him, telling him to hide. He also promised David that he would speak to his father and would let David know what he learned.

Scene 2 (19:4-7)

As he said he would, Jonathan talked to his father. "David put his life on the line against the Philistine army, and God delivered Israel," Jonathan reminded Saul. "You rejoiced in the victory. Why would you sin by killing David without good reason? He is innocent."

Saul listened to his son and dropped his plan to kill David. Jonathan reported the good news to David and brought him back into the king's presence, where he resumed his position as the captain of Saul's bodyguard—and military commander as needed.

Scene 3 (19:8-10)

David picked up where he left off, going back out to defeat the Philistines again. His "reward" from Saul was having the king hurl his spear at him.[69] David ducked out of the way and escaped to his house.

Scene 4 (19:11-17)

Saul didn't give up. He sent "messengers" (hit men) to David's house with instructions to kill David. But David's wife Michal knew (or suspected) the king's plan, so she helped David get away during the night, letting him down through a window. Then she fixed the bed to make it appear that David was in it; when Saul's messengers came to the house, Michal said that David was ill. But Saul discovered the ruse, and he confronted Michal, who was his daughter. "Why have you deceived me?" Saul said to Michal.

---

69   Saul was tormented by an "evil spirit from the Lord," perhaps to convict him, perhaps in judgment of his disobedience. See, New Spirit-Filled Bible, New King James Version (Thomas Nelson Bibles, Nashville, TN 2003), note to 1 Samuel 16:14.

"He said he would kill me if I didn't," she replied.

Act 2 (1 Samuel 19:18-24)

David showed up at Samuel's place in Ramah[70] and told him his story. (David knew Samuel because Samuel had called him from his father's field, anointing him as the future king.) Samuel took David to stay with him in Naioth (a part of Ramah) where there was a school of prophets. It seemed like a safe place, but Saul's "messengers" weren't far behind. When Saul's men reached Naioth, however, they found that the prophets, with Samuel presiding, were prophesying (speaking the word of God and praising the Lord). Instead of looking for David, the messengers themselves started prophesying, the Spirit of the Lord having come upon them! Saul sent a second contingent of messengers; they prophesied too! The same thing happened to a third wave of messengers. Desperate enough to abandon the conventional wisdom that a king should let others do his dirty work, Saul himself came to Naioth; he, too, prophesied! With his pursuers under the Holy Spirit's control, David was able to get away.

Act 3 (1 Samuel 20)

Scene 1 (20:1-11)

David returned home and went to Jonathan, puzzled. "What have I done?" he asked. "What is my sin?"

---

70   The exact location of Ramah (known as Arimathea in New Testament times) is not known, but it is thought to be several miles from Gibeah, Saul's birthplace and the capitol of his kingdom. Gibeah was about three miles north of Jerusalem.

"You will not die," Jonathan encouraged him, "my father does nothing without telling me, and I will see that you are safe."

But David wasn't convinced. "The truth is, I am only a step away from death," he said. "Tell me what I can do for you," Jonathan begged.

Then David proposed a plan. David would hide in a field while Jonathan returned to the palace to attend the New Moon celebration.[71] Jonathan would watch for Saul's reaction to David's absence from the table. "If your father notices my absence, tell him that I had asked permission to go to Bethlehem because of the yearly sacrifice there for my family," David proposed. "If he approves, then I will be safe, but if he is angry, then I will know he still wants to kill me."

Then Jonathan reassured David. "If my father plotted evil, would I not tell you?" he said.

Scene 2 (20:12-23)

Then the two went out into the field where David would hide. There they worked out the details of the plan for Jonathan to communicate the king's response. Jonathan continued to reassure David; he told David that he wanted to take the hit if he did not warn David of any plan by the king to kill him. "If my father intends to do you harm, then let me be harmed if I do not warn you," Jonathan said. Jonathan and David agreed to demonstrate the Lord's love and kindness to each other and their families,

---

71   Israel celebrated the Festival of the New Moon, a time to be enjoyed but also a time to dedicate the next month to God. Life Application Bible, The Living Bible Translation (Tyndale House Publishers, Wheaton, IL 1988), note to 1 Samuel 20:5.

affirming that their commitment to each other was based on their commitment to God. "Our Lord is between you and me forever," Jonathan said.

Scene 3 (20:24-34)

"Where is David?" Saul asked the second night of the feast. Jonathan gave the explanation that he and David had previously agreed to. It wasn't the answer Saul wanted. Boiling with rage, Saul focused his anger on Jonathan. "I know that you want that son of a nobody to be king, shaming your mother and me," Saul yelled. "You will never be king as long as he is alive. Now bring him to me so I can kill him."

When Jonathan asked, "Why, what did he do?" the king tried to kill his son. Now it was Jonathan's turn to be angry, and he left the table.

Scene 4 (20:35-42)

Jonathan went back to the field where David was hiding. Responding to a prearranged signal, David came out of his hiding place and greeted Jonathan. They wept, knowing that they had to say goodbye. "Go in safety," Jonathan told his friend, "and be of good cheer, because we have entrusted each other and our children into God's hands."[72] So they parted, Jonathan returning to the city.

Act 4 (1 Samuel 21:1-9)

David's next stop was Nob, a short distance from Jerusalem, where he found Ahimelech the priest. After telling the priest that he was on a secret mission from the king, David asked for something

---

72   1 Samuel 20:42 (TLB)

to eat. All the priest had was the bread of the Presence—which was to be eaten only by the priests—but he gave it to David. When David asked for a spear or sword—explaining that he left in such a hurry on the king's mission that he didn't grab a weapon—the priest gave him the sword of Goliath, whom David had killed. Evidently, Ahimelech prayed to the Lord on David's behalf before giving him the food and weapon.[73]

Epilogue

Fearing that Saul would catch up with him (Saul had resumed the chase), David traveled to Gath, which was some distance away. But Gath was a Philistine stronghold, and when he arrived, the people recognized David as the leader of the enemy's (Israel's) army. Thinking that he might be harmed, David feigned insanity, and Gath's king Achish sent him away. With Saul still in pursuit, David hid in the cave of Adullum, where relatives joined him. David continued on the move, passing up several opportunities to kill Saul, but Saul was eventually killed by the Philistines. Unfortunately, Jonathan was killed in the same battle. David was made king and later took time to care for Jonathan's lame son[74]—according to David's covenant promise to Jonathan and his family.

Thoughts for the Chaplain

This story has four chaplains—Jonathan, Michal, Samuel, and Ahimelech. Each acted independently, and each made a different contribution to David's well-being. Collectively, their actions

---

73   1 Samuel 22:13,15

74   2 Samuel 9:1-13

provide guidance to chaplains—and raise some significant ethical and spiritual issues for chaplains to consider.

The decision as to whether to help a person in distress can be a difficult one. This was especially true in Jonathan's case. If he helped David, he would not only be disobeying his father but also challenging the authority of the king. The latter act could, in some circumstances at least, get a person killed. Consider also that David's death would put Jonathan in line to succeed Saul as king (at least in Saul's thinking). Yet Jonathan was devoted to David. Further, he believed that killing David would be against God's laws. The deciding factor for Jonathan, therefore, seemed to be: *what is right in God's eyes?* To Jonathan, acting in love for a friend was more important than obtaining personal gain, and saving David's life was worth the risk connected with disobeying his father, the king. Jonathan may have defied conventional (human) wisdom in becoming David's protector and advocate, but he believed that he was following God's wisdom as chaplains are called to do.

Of course, David was a friend of Jonathan; chaplains typically are called on to minister to people they do not know. But, as the story of the Good Samaritan (chapter 1) shows, everyone is our neighbor, and we are to love and serve them all.

A chaplain is called to put others first even if there is risk (within limits). Whether acting out of loyalty to a friend (as did Jonathan), through commitment as a spouse (as did Michal), or merely carrying out one's duty as a chaplain, serving another who is in distress can involve risk to the chaplain. Jonathan took a chance when he told David of Saul's plan to kill him, but Jonathan did not see an option: "Let me be harmed if I do not warn you," Jonathan said. He didn't stop there. He increased his personal risk by confronting his father openly as an advocate for David, and his father nearly killed him as a result. Michal risked the anger of her father when she helped David escape.

Ahimelech the priest lost his life because he helped David. A spy for the king reported what transpired at Nob, and Saul summoned Ahimelech. Although Ahimelech explained why he had no reason to believe that David was running from the king and that he knew nothing of a plot to kill Saul, the king nevertheless ordered the killing of Ahimelech, his family, and the other priests who served at Nob. Saul acted, in part, because—according to him—Ahimelech knew that David was fleeing, but did not report it to the king.[75]

We may not face death when we serve as chaplains—in fact, chaplains are warned not to risk their lives unnecessarily—but we may nevertheless encounter risk of illness, physical exhaustion, injury, and psychological burnout as a result of chaplain activities.

We can encounter difficult spiritual and ethical issues as we minister to others. The issues include:

Whether to disobey civil authority.

Jonathan refused to comply with the king's order because he believed that killing David would violate God's law. God's word requires that we obey civil leaders. However, there may be circumstances in which we would be justified in disobeying an order or denying a request. If we are asked to violate God's law, for example, we—like Jonathan—might be justified in saying "no." Similarly, we might reject a directive that would require us to transgress man's

---

75   1 Samuel 22:9-19

law. For example, a military service member is not required to obey an unlawful order of a commanding officer.

Whether to break God's rule.

David asked Ahimelech for something to eat, but the only food available was the holy bread that was to be eaten only by the priests.[76] Nevertheless, Ahimelech put David's need above a legalistic application of the Levitical law. Jesus referred with approval to the priest's decision when he confronted the Pharisees who protested that his disciples were breaking the law against the Sabbath when they harvested grain to satisfy their hunger.[77] "I want you to be merciful more than I want your offerings," [78] Jesus told them.

Whether to lie and practice deception.

When, if ever, is it okay to lie (or deceive) to protect someone? Jonathan didn't tell the truth when he gave Saul the excuse for David's absence from the feast. Michal lied twice—first, when she said that David was ill, and second, when she told Saul that David had threatened to kill her. We might readily attempt to protect our spouse or another family member in similar ways. But what about others? Should we lie or deceive to hide an illegal alien from immigration authorities? If we are sheltering a battered wife, we might lie to the abusive husband by telling him we don't know where his wife is. Would a better answer be, "I refuse to discuss the matter"? We might not be inclined to lie or deceive to protect someone if a policeman or deputy sheriff were looking to arrest the person. But

---

76   Leviticus 24:5-9, Exodus 25:30

77   Matthew 12:1-8. Verses 3 and 4 refer to the incident involving David and Ahimelech.

78   Matthew 12:7 (TLB)

what if we know that the authorities would be acting unlawfully if they made the arrest?

Can we justify lying to someone who intends to violate God's or man's law by reasoning that he is not entitled to the truth? In all the circumstances we have discussed, is it better not to lie or deceive, but instead prayerfully to leave the matter to the wisdom of God?

There are many references to lying and deceit in the Bible, and plenty of verses tell of God's dim view of those practices. We start, of course, with the ninth commandment: "You shall not bear false witness against your neighbor."[79] It doesn't list any exceptions! We will not attempt to do an in-depth analysis of Scripture on this matter but instead suggest a careful study of His Word and Bible-based commentary to guide you.[80] There is plenty of grist for discussion!

There are different ways to help someone who needs protection. Jonathan and the other chaplains protected David from Saul's threatened action that would have violated God's law against murder. Obviously, a chaplain may put himself in legal jeopardy if he harbors a fugitive from justice. But there will be times when a chaplain legitimately can help someone who is threatened with harm physically or emotionally.

A chaplain may offer shelter, food, and other necessities to a person in distress—as did Ahimelech and Samuel in David's case. And the chaplain may offer emotional support, as did Jonathan in response to David's despair. Jonathan addressed David's worries

---

79   Exodus 20:16

80   See, for example, Charles C. Ryrie, *Biblical Answers to Contemporary Issues,* (Moody Press: Chicago, 1991), Chapter 6, *The Question of Situational Ethics.*

and reminded David that his actions to protect David were based on their covenant before God. Of course, bringing the person to an organization or agency that will provide shelter and protection may be the appropriate action to take.

Jonathan did what he promised to do; his reliability surely supported David's emotional condition. Finally, Ahimelech served David by praying for him (he "consulted the Lord"[81]), something that chaplains can always do for those they serve.

Saying goodbye to those we have served can be difficult. Jonathan and David said a tearful goodbye in the field, and they parted not knowing whether they would see each other again. In the same way, chaplains may experience sadness as they leave those whom they have served, as well as those with whom they have served (fellow chaplains and other coworkers). Chaplains often develop friendships as well as spiritual relationships with those they have helped. We may regret leaving people who remain in difficult circumstances, while we return to family and friends in a comfortable environment.

This was the situation for David and Jonathan when they separated for the last time; they comforted themselves in the knowledge of their covenant to one another and their families, and of God's everlasting covenant with those who follow Him. Consolation for the chaplain and the one served may come in the chaplain's commitment to continue to pray for the other person, to follow-up with a phone call or other communication, or—as circumstances permit—to return for face-to-face ministry.

---

81   1 Samuel 22:15. See Matthew Henry, op. cit., Vol. II, p. 400

Chapter 11

SOLVING A MAJOR PROBLEM IN THE FACE OF MAJOR OPPOSITION

Nehemiah, the Full Service Leader-Chaplain
The Book of Nehemiah

THE OPPOSITION CAME IN A variety of ways, one wave right after another. Some people began to believe that the goal—building a wall to protect the people in Jerusalem—could not be achieved. The leader of the project could well have become discouraged and might have given up on the ambitious project.

But for this particular leader, a man named Nehemiah, quitting was simply not an option. He believed fervently that the God of heaven had called him to the task and that He wanted Nehemiah to finish it. Nehemiah had been going about his business as a cupbearer[82] to king Artaxerxes—Nehemiah was one of the people of Israel who were living in exile in the Persian Empire—when news that energized Nehemiah arrived.

"The wall around Jerusalem is broken down," a delegation that included Nehemiah's brother reported to Nehemiah, "and the gates have been burned. The people are in great distress." This was indeed tragic news, because the Israelites who were living in Jerusalem—after having been allowed to return to the city in earlier years—needed the wall for protection from their enemies. Jerusalem was in Judah, which was a province in the Persian Empire, although it was not defended by the king's soldiers.

When Nehemiah heard the devastating news, he "sat down and wept and mourned for days and fasted and prayed [constantly] before the God of heaven."[83] He confessed that he and all the people of Israel had sinned. He acknowledged that God had warned the people that if they were unfaithful, they would be scattered among the nations, but God had also encouraged them with the word that if they repented, He would bring them to His chosen place (Jerusalem). Then Nehemiah prayed that God would grant him compassion before the king as he approached the king with a request.

"Why do you have a long face?" the king asked Nehemiah.

"It's because the place where my ancestors are buried has been desolated," Nehemiah replied.

---

82   A cupbearer selected and tasted the king's wine to make sure that it was not poisoned. It was a responsible position, one that gave the cupbearer access to, and influence with, the king.

83   Nehemiah 1:4 (Amplified Bible)

"What are you asking for?" the king wanted to know.

Nehemiah breathed a prayer and responded, "Send me to rebuild the city."

"Done," said the king, and he gave Nehemiah the written authority he needed, including the right to take timber from the king's forest to rebuild Jerusalem's gates, safe passage through the royal provinces, and appointment as Jerusalem's governor. At the king's request, Nehemiah gave him a date for his return to the king's palace. The trip from the palace in Susa[84]—located in modern Iran, near the border with Iraq at the top of the Persian Gulf—would take several months, but that was not a problem for the motivated Nehemiah.

"The good hand of God was on me," Nehemiah wrote, explaining the reason for the king's favor. But Sanballat and Tobiah, leaders from nearby Samaria and Ammon—who benefited by Jerusalem's weakness—heard of the plans, and they were not happy.

Nehemiah knew that he needed to hide his plans from these enemies as much as possible. He later wrote that after he arrived in Jerusalem, "I did not tell anyone what my God was telling me to do for the city." He made a nighttime tour of what was left of the wall and then went to the city officials with a simple proposal: "Let us rebuild the wall of Jerusalem."

The officials were receptive. "Let us arise and build," they said. So they got started. It was to be no small task since the wall was about two miles long.[85] The Israelites who had returned

---

84   Susa is thought by some to have been the king's winter capitol.

85   The exact height and width are not known, but the wall, which was made of stone, may have been as high as 15 feet or more and a number of feet

to Jerusalem over the previous century had been unable to restore the wall, although they had rebuilt the temple that was inside the remnants of the wall.

Sanballat and Tobiah, joined by Geshem (a powerful leader of Arabian tribes), were right there, accusing the Jews in Jerusalem of rebelling against Artaxerxes. "God will give us success, so we are going to build," Nehemiah responded, adding that "you have no right to be in this city." Nehemiah made sure that the people of Jerusalem were assigned responsibilities, and they pitched in to rebuild the wall and its gates.

Realizing that they had not intimidated Nehemiah, and motivated by anger, the opposition pulled the ridicule weapon out of their armory. The enemies mocked and belittled the building program, calling the Jews "feeble," unable to build a sturdy wall. "If a fox jumped on the wall, he would break it down," Tobiah scoffed.

Nehemiah went to God, acknowledged that the enemies' actions angered Him, and asked that He punish the interlopers for demoralizing the workers. And the building continued, "for the people had a mind to work,"[86] with Nehemiah pitching in to do his share.

When the wall was half built, the detractors, who were now joined by the Ashdodites, upgraded from angry to very angry. Ready to take their campaign to the next level, they conspired to launch a secret attack on Jerusalem. Learning of the planned assault, the Jews prayed to their God and set up a guard day and night. Yet the workers, who were tired, became discouraged by the rumors of

---

thick.

86   Nehemiah 4:6

imminent attack. Then, when the laborers heard that the enemies planned to sneak into Jerusalem and kill them without warning, they became fearful.

Nehemiah strengthened the defenses and reassured the people. "Do not be afraid," Nehemiah told them, "remember the Lord who is great and awesome, and fight for your families." God had frustrated the enemies' plan for a secret attack, so they stayed away, and the people returned to work. But the workers remained vigilant— some carried a load of building materials with one hand and their weapon with the other. Nehemiah arranged for trumpeters to provide warning of an impending attack and instructed the guards to be ready at all times. And all were armed with the Word of the Lord! And the enemy continued to stay away.

Unfortunately, not all the threats came from enemies outside the city. There was a food shortage in the city; some of the Jews bought grain from other Jews but were required to mortgage their own properties in return for the grain. Some borrowed money from their Israelite brothers to pay the taxes imposed by the Persian rulers but were charged exorbitant interest rates; to repay their creditors, they had to sell their children into slavery.[87] All this created turmoil that threatened to stop the building.

Nehemiah was angry. But after time for reflection (he wrote that he "consulted with himself"), he took constructive action. He rebuked those who violated God's commandment not to charge their own people interest. He called a meeting to point out that he and others had set the example by redeeming some of their brothers

---

87   "The Bible Knowledge Commentary, " *op. cit., New Testament, p.* 657

who had been sold to foreigners. Nehemiah added that he did not take the governor's food allowance but shared it with others without requiring mortgages in return. He reminded the people that God's reputation was at stake and that they would be seen as hypocritical if they did not follow His laws. Then he asked the people to return the property and interest payments they had taken from others. The people listened to Nehemiah and promised to stop their unacceptable behavior.[88]

The attack from without continued, this time with subtle deceit. When the wall was built, but the gates not yet in place, the enemies called Nehemiah to a meeting—presumably a peace conference—at a location some twenty or more miles away from Jerusalem, a place that bordered on hostile territory. Knowing that they planned to harm him, Nehemiah replied that he couldn't stop his work. The enemies were persistent: they made the same proposal three more times, and each time Nehemiah responded in the same way.

Sanballat didn't give up. He sent a fifth message, this one reporting rumors that accused Nehemiah and the other Jews of planning to rebel and set up Nehemiah as the king of Jerusalem. "The king is going to learn about this," Sanballat said, "so we had better talk." Nehemiah's reply was blunt. "You're making this up," he said. Realizing that the enemy was again trying to frighten the workers, Nehemiah prayed, "O God, strengthen my hands."

One final challenge involved treachery by a person on the inside. A man named Shemaiah approached Nehemiah and told him that his enemies were coming to kill him at night. Shemaiah offered a solution. "Let us go into the temple and close the doors," he

---

said. Nehemiah refused. Nehemiah perceived that God had not sent the man to warn him but that Tobiah and Sanballat had hired him to lure Nehemiah into the temple. Entering the temple would have been a sin for Nehemiah; only the priests were allowed in the temple, and—since no one would have come to try to kill him—Nehemiah would have been disgraced. So the plot failed.

The workers finished the wall, complete with gates, fifty-two days after the work started. Jerusalem was open for safe living again, and more people could return from exile. The enemies were disheartened, losing their confidence[89] and acknowledging that God was responsible for the success of the project. But Nehemiah, knowing that the enemy was still around—for example, Tobiah (who had family ties to the Israelites) continued to send threatening letters—devised a security system to protect the people.

Nehemiah appointed faithful, God-fearing leaders for Jerusalem since he had to return to the king's palace as he had promised. Then Ezra, who had traveled to Jerusalem fourteen years before Nehemiah arrived, came to read the law to the people, making sure that the people understood the Word of the Lord their God. The people observed a sacred day, worshipped in joy—"the joy of the Lord is your strength,"[90] they were told—and celebrated the Feast of Tabernacles.[91] The people responded with weeping and repentance. They ratified their covenant with God. They repopulated

---

89   "They were much cast down in their own eyes..." (Nehemiah 6:16, King James Version)

90   Nehemiah 8:10

91   The Feast of Tabernacles was a commemoration of God's goodness in leading the people out of Egypt and through the wilderness.

the cities surrounding Jerusalem. They rededicated the wall. They instituted reforms in several areas of their society. And Nehemiah closed the book with:

Remember me, O God, for good.

Nehemiah 13:31

Thoughts for the Chaplain

Nehemiah is an outstanding biblical example of a full service leader-chaplain. He saw the need to help people in distress; took steps to put himself in a position both to lead and serve; inspired the people to undertake the task ("they had a mind to work"); helped organize the effort; pitched in to do his share; took leadership in dealing with the opposition; and reassured the people when the going got tough. Nehemiah's actions are often cited as examples of leadership. But a major part of his effort in Jerusalem also meets our definition of a chaplain: he ministered to people who were in distress, helping them meet physical and emotional needs. He encouraged those who were doing the physical work to restore the wall, much as some of today's chaplains minister to those who are rebuilding damaged houses. Thus, his story provides much in the way of inspiration and guidance to chaplains.

Never, never give up, no matter how many times the enemy attacks. Nehemiah knew the cause was right because he knew that God wanted the people to return to Judah and Jerusalem. So he acted in unwavering, unconditional faith that God would see the project through. When the enemy attacked, he turned to God, encouraged the workers to remember His greatness, and faced down the enemy on several occasions.

As the building progressed, the number of enemies increased, and the threats accelerated. Nehemiah and the people of Jerusalem survived threats that slanderous reports would be made to Artaxerxes as well as intimidation from imminent physical attack, ridicule, and a plot to lure him out of the city where he would be harmed. And those were just the attacks from the outside! The enemy outside the walls was subtle and sophisticated—but notice that the attacks never moved from psychological warfare to physical warfare. Nehemiah and his people called their bluffs.

There are times when Satan's attacks bring fatigue and discouragement to chaplains, and thoughts of giving up a particular effort occur. We (the authors) have experienced those times. We have found great comfort in what has become one of our theme verses: "Let us not lose heart in doing good, for in due time we will reap if we do not grow weary."[92] By pressing on despite the attacks, we call Satan's bluff.

Be prepared for challenges from within, including problems with the very people we are trying to help. Unfortunately, Satan works not only through the enemy but also through those who we are working to help. These problems can threaten to disrupt or ruin our efforts to help the people. Nehemiah confronted the financial extortion problems in a timely manner, ending a situation that could have led to dissension that would have stopped the building project. And, when one of the Jews joined with the enemy in an attempt to disgrace Nehemiah, with God's help Nehemiah saw through the effort to cause him to sin by entering the temple. Nehemiah knew that he needed to be wary when he was asked to do something that would violate God's law (enter the temple). "Will it violate God's law?" is a good question for chaplains to raise when they are asked to do something that appears to be questionable.

Prepare for the ministry; plan ahead. Nehemiah prepared for the mission, first, by approaching divine authority. Weeping and mourning, he went to God in prayer, asking for His favor. Then, he went to earthly authority with a plan in mind. Before Nehemiah approached the king, he considered what the king would need to know—for example, when Nehemiah would return to the palace from his wall-building mission. He was also prepared to ask for the specific written authority he would need from the king for building materials and safe passage. As soon as he arrived in Jerusalem, Nehemiah gathered information about the status of the wall through his nighttime reconnaissance before proposing the building project. His foresight guided the project to the finish.

Keep focused on the task. Nehemiah could have been distracted by the enemy without and the problems within. Since he was the lead builder, the project could have foundered had his attention been diverted. But he kept focused. "I have work to do," he told Sanballat. "Go away!" We cannot let anyone—man or Satan—sidetrack us from our main goal.

Prayer is vitally important. Nehemiah was never far away from his God, humbling himself through prayer right from the start when he learned of the problem in Jerusalem. His prayer of confession opened the door to God's mercy. He prayed that the king would have a compassionate heart when he heard Nehemiah's request.

When the building project was threatened, he prayed that God would punish the attackers. He prayed for strength to finish the project when it was nearing completion. Sometimes his prayers were short ("O God, strengthen my hand") and discreet (he prayed silently as he approached the king with his request); at other times, they were longer as circumstances permitted. And his prayers were answered—including his opening prayer for repentance on the part of the people, which happened after the wall was built and the people heard the reading of God's Word. And Nehemiah gave God the glory for everything, for example, "the good hand of God was on me" when the king approved his request.

Encouragement is at the core of the chaplain's service. If any of Nehemiah's behavior throughout the story was chaplain-like, it was his encouragement (along with prayer). Whatever the problem, Nehemiah was there to lift the people up. An example occurred when the people became tired, discouraged, and fearful after learning of the enemy's plot to attack the builders. Nehemiah responded with words, reminding the people that God would protect them, and with action (strengthening the defenses, setting up a warning system, and instructing the guards to be on the alert).

Wisdom is essential during times of continuing challenge. Wisdom has many facets, as illustrated by the book of Nehemiah.

- Wisdom means pausing at crucial times to ask for God's guidance. When the king asked what Nehemiah wanted, he breathed a quick prayer first instead of blurting out his request. When Nehemiah learned of the financial extortion within the city, he waited until his anger subsided before taking action.

- Wisdom means being prudent. Knowing that enemies were watching, Nehemiah made his first inspection of the wall alone and at night, so the enemies could not stop the project before it got started. He also instructed some of the workers to work with one hand and carry a weapon with another.

- Wisdom means being vigilant. Nehemiah set up guards and arranged for trumpeters to provide warning.   Each time the project reached a benchmark—completion of half of the wall, completion of the wall but not the gates—the enemy ramped up its efforts, but Nehemiah had the people ready to respond.

- Wisdom means having discernment. Nehemiah knew when an invitation to negotiate could lead to his harm, and he discerned that the advice to seek refuge in the temple was a trap.

- Wisdom means paying careful attention to the enemy's action. When Sanballat made the offer for a peace conference five times without changing the proposed meeting place, Nehemiah knew that Sanballat was more interested in getting Nehemiah far away from Jerusalem than in having meaningful negotiations.

- Wisdom means knowing how to approach the other person. Nehemiah was tactful and courteous when he spoke to the king. Sometimes he gave respectful answers to his enemies, but he knew when to give a direct, blunt reply to deter the enemy—for example, "you have no right to be in this city" and "you are making this up!"

Wisdom is available for the asking: "if any of you lacks wisdom, let him ask of God."[93]

We may need to take risks. Nehemiah went to the king with sadness in his face; that was enough to get a person killed in those days, for those who approached the king were required to be (or at least appear to be) happy. The king had previously ordered construction in Jerusalem to cease; requesting that he lift the moratorium could arouse his anger. (Wisely, he did not use the word "Jerusalem" before the king, appealing instead to the king's respect for burial grounds.) Obviously, Nehemiah took many risks after he arrived in Jerusalem, but he pushed ahead courageously nevertheless.

A positive witness for God is essential. Twice during the story Nehemiah illustrated the importance of not appearing to be hypocrites to those outside the faith. First, he reminded the people who were involved in the financial misdeeds that God's reputation was at stake. (Note that Nehemiah turned down some of the perks that were available to someone in his position, for example, by sharing the governor's food allowance; chaplains can set a similar example by the lifestyles they portray when they serve those who have little.) Then, his refusal to enter the temple avoided criticism that he, as the leader, did not really follow the God he professed to obey. We cannot give Satan an opportunity to discredit our God.

> *So the wall was completed ... in fifty-two days...when all our enemies heard of it ... they recognized that this work had been accomplished with the help of our God.*
>
> Neh. 6:15–16

---

93   James 1:5

Chapter 12

A LIFE OR DEATH DECISION "FOR SUCH A TIME AS THIS"

The Story of Esther
The Book of Esther

THE QUEEN WAS FACED WITH a major dilemma. Under the king's authority, an influential palace official named Haman had issued letters authorizing the killing of her people—Jews—who lived in the kingdom.[94] The king, Ahasuerus,[95] had great authority, ruling over a vast territory (the Persian Empire) stretching from modern Pakistan to northern Africa. Those acting under his authority had the power to assure that the death order would be carried out

---

94   The Jews' ancestors had been brought into Persia by Nebuchadnezzar, who captured Jerusalem more than a century earlier. Persia was now ruled by Ahasuerus.

95   Ahasuerus was also known as Xerxes.

according to the letters that were delivered to all of the many provinces in the empire.

The queen, whose name was Esther, had learned the terrible news from her cousin Mordecai, whose family had raised her.[96] Mordecai was not only the bearer of bad news; he was the immediate cause of the king's decree. Using the excuse that he was a Jew, Mordecai refused to bow down to Haman, who was the number two man in the Ahasuerus administration.[97] This offended Haman, who then got the king to authorize the order without telling him which people were to be destroyed. (The king may have been more interested in Haman's promise to put ten thousand talents of silver into the royal treasury to pay for the cost of the extermination campaign.)[98]

Understandably, both Esther and Mordecai were greatly distressed over the decree. If the decree were to be fully enforced, the two of them would die along with all their relatives and the rest of the Jews who lived in the empire. "You have to go to the king and plead for the lives of the Jews," Mordecai told Esther.

Mordecai's request created the queen's dilemma. If she went to the king without a summons from him, she might be killed,

---

96   Mordecai sat at the king's gate, possibly as an official appointed by Esther.

97   The Jews would ordinarily bow down to the captors, but Mordecai would not in this case, possibly because Haman claimed that he was a divine being.

98   Haman may have intended to pay the money from his own wealth or from plunder taken from the Jews. The amount promised was about twelve million ounces of silver.

because no one—not even the queen—was permitted to approach the king except at his request. "You could be killed anyway because you are a Jew," her cousin argued, "so what do you have to lose?" Mordecai added, "God will find a way to save the Jews if you don't" —referring, apparently, to God's promise to Israel's leaders starting with Abraham that He would save His chosen people. But the nation of Israel would have to be preserved through Jews living outside the Persian Empire if Haman's decree was enforced.

So Mordecai immediately posed an intriguing question to Esther: "What if you have become royalty *for such a time as this?*" In other words, "what if God has brought you, Esther, to this time and place so that you could be His instrument for saving His people?"

Esther reflected on her unlikely rise to royalty. She had been an insignificant orphaned Jew living in a land ruled by Gentiles. Through an unusual circumstance, she had been selected along with hundreds of others as candidates to replace queen Vashti. (The king had divorced Vashti because she refused to appear at a king's banquet so that her beauty would be on display before the princes and other guests. Ordinarily the new queen would have been selected from among the princes' daughters. In this case, however, the princes— thinking that the king was considering bringing Vashti back to the throne and suspecting that she would have them killed because of their role in the divorce—suggested that the new queen be selected from the most beautiful virgins in the kingdom.) And the king selected Esther from all the candidates.

Maybe cousin Mordecai was right—maybe God had selected her to be the one to save the Jews. On the other hand, if she didn't intervene, she might still be spared even though the other Jews in the kingdom would be killed. So far, she had hidden her ancestry from the king and his authorities; even if her heritage was revealed, the king might protect her because she was the queen. But what would happen to Mordecai and his family?

In theory, Esther may have had some time to make her decision. By casting lots, Haman had determined that the killings would not begin for eleven months. But she didn't need much time to conclude that she would try to help her people. "Tell the Jews to fast for me," she instructed Mordecai. "I will go to the king. *If I die, I die.*"

Esther approached the king, and he accepted her presence. That hurdle was past. The king even seemed anxious to accommodate her. "What is troubling you?" he asked. She didn't come right to the point. Instead, she asked the king to have Haman join the two of them at a banquet that she had prepared. There, when the king inquired about her request, she deferred again, asking only for another banquet the following day. The king agreed.

Haman left the palace pumped up. After all, he had been the only guest at a royal banquet—a rare honor. But then he passed Mordecai, who again refused to bow down to him. When he got home, Haman bragged to his wife and friends about his invitation to back-to-back banquets. Then he told them how Mordecai's insubordination brought him down.

"Build a gallows to hang Mordecai on," his wife and friends advised. "Hang him tomorrow, and then join the king in the banquet."

"Great idea," responded Haman. "I can get rid of him now instead of waiting to have him killed with all the other Jews." So

Haman's workers built the gallows—75 feet high, nearly as high as the city walls; Haman wanted all to see the body of the disgraced man.

When night fell on the royal palace, the king could not get to sleep. So he asked someone to read from the king's book of records. The reader turned to the page that reported the story of an incident, several years earlier, in which Mordecai had interrupted a plot to kill the king. The king wanted to know whether Mordecai had been properly honored; the answer was "no."

The next day, just as Haman was about to seek the king's permission for the hanging of Mordecai, the king asked Haman, "what should I do to honor a man who truly pleases me?" Thinking that the king had him in mind, Haman described a ceremony that included putting the man in royal robes, crowning him with the royal crown, mounting him on the king's own horse, and having a royal prince lead the horse through the streets.

"Excellent," the king said. "You do it to Mordecai."

Uh-oh. Haman had no choice; he was forced to honor Mordecai in the city square. Haman went home in shame, where his friends warned him that his plan to kill the Jews was history. Then Haman was summoned to the banquet with the king and queen.

"What is your request?" the king again asked Esther at the banquet.

"Spare me and my people," she answered, telling the king about the fate that awaited the Jews.

The king was stunned. "Who was responsible for the order to kill the Jews?" he demanded to know. "Who would touch you?"

Another hurdle had been passed; the king would defend Esther as a Jew. Esther answered the king: "Haman is the man," she said.

Angry, the king retreated to his garden, returning just as Haman—who had approached Esther to plead for his life—fell on the couch where she was reclining. Taking the worst possible interpretation of the scene, the king ordered that Haman be hanged on the gallows Haman had built for Mordecai. And it was done.

The king quickly gave Mordecai authority to countermand the letters that Haman had issued for the destruction of the Jews.[99] Mordecai's letters granted the Jews the right to assemble and protect themselves, which was necessary because some of the Persians had prematurely attacked them under the Haman decree. The Jews were able to defeat those who threatened them, killing many, including Haman's ten sons who were—fittingly—hanged on the gallows. At the direction of Mordecai and Esther, the Jews began to celebrate God's goodness during two days each month in what became known as the Feast of Purim. The king honored Mordecai and made him second in command in his empire—giving him Haman's old job!

Thoughts for the Chaplain

Was Esther serving as a chaplain when she acted to save her people? Technically, maybe not. She did not minister directly to the people. Yet, the story of what she—and Mordecai—did illustrates principles that go to the heart of what the chaplaincy is all about.

---

99   Under the law, Haman's decree—having been issued under the king's authority—could not be reversed. But Mordecai, also acting under the king's authority, could issue orders that, in effect, nullified Haman's orders.

God may be calling us to serve "for such a time as this," but uncertainty and risk may complicate the decision whether to answer the call. If Esther goes to the king, she might be killed just for approaching him, but if not, then the Jews in the empire might be spared. On the other hand, if she doesn't act, the Jews likely would die. She might be among those to die, but then maybe Mordecai was wrong— perhaps her life would be spared because she was the queen.

Notice the "may," the "mights," the "maybe" and the "likely"— all words of uncertainty that complicate a decision.

In the end, Esther resolved the doubts by choosing the option (going to the king) that gave her people the best chance of escaping total destruction—an unselfish choice, since electing the other option might have improved her chance of survival. It really came down to this: the overriding point from Esther's perspective was Mordecai's intriguing statement that maybe she was the one appointed "for such a time as this." Esther rightly decided that, under the circumstances, she was the one to do His work.

The statement that Esther was confronted with is one that has inspired and challenged Christians through the years: "Perhaps God has brought me here for such a time as this." In other words, maybe I am the right person at the right time to do something that God wants done. Maybe it is my life's purpose in His eyes. Each of us likely will encounter one or more "for such a time as this" moments in our lives—times when we might reflect on the events in our lives as we decide whether, like Esther, God has brought us to a certain place so that we might do a specific part of His work.

We may not encounter the "such a time as this" challenge in a life-or-death context, as did Esther. Perhaps people would not die if we refuse God's calling, as might have happened in Esther's case. But, as one of our Bible study members observed, we might experience a death in our spirit if we say "no" to God. And there might be other negative consequences, such as the needs of some people going unmet if others are not there to serve in our place. Obviously, we cannot respond to every request, and there are many times when God can use someone else. But other times when God calls, He is not looking for the response of "someone else will do it if I don't."

The consequences of a decision to get involved can be severe, but God may want us to take the risk. Esther knew that she was risking her life by going to see the king. But she also knew that she had to do it, and that she had to accept the risk: "If I die, I die." This may seem like a fatalistic statement, but it also can be seen as an expression of confidence in God's will and wisdom. That is, "God, if it is in your wisdom and is in accordance with your will that I die, then I accept it." Again, we might not be called into situations where our lives are at risk—though God may call us to be willing to love others to the point of sacrificing our lives: "We know love by this, that He laid down His life for us; and we ought to lay down our lives for the brethren." 1 John 3:16. Even if our lives are not on the line, there may be risk of another kind—be it health, financial, or otherwise—that God wants us to undertake, carrying with us His promise that He will never leave us or forsake us.[100]

Having a trusted advisor can make it easier to reach the right decision. Mordecai not only advised Esther to do that which—at least in his mind—needed to be done. He also helped focus her thinking

---

100   God made this promise to believers in Hebrews 13:5, and to Joshua (Joshua 1:5) as well as to all Israel (Deuteronomy 31:6).

toward what her decision should be based on. And he remained available to Esther, staying at the king's gate throughout the entire episode. Esther listened to Mordecai. Solomon wrote that "wisdom is found in those who take advice." [101]

Prayer is essential not only when a decision is being made but also in the implementation. Esther announced her decision to approach the king no matter the consequences and at the same time asked for fasting on her behalf. The focus at that point was on the success of her effort, the decision having been made. Although Esther did not use the word "prayer" when she called for the fast,[102] undoubtedly prayer was to be at the heart of the fasting. Furthermore, Esther didn't limit the call to a few people close to her; she asked that all the people who could be mobilized for the fast—all the Jews in Susa—participate. And even though prompt action to head off the slaughter of the Jews was needed, Esther made sure to allow plenty of time (three days) for the first priority—fasting and getting prayed up.

God may want us to get involved even if the people we help (and we, ourselves) have not been obedient to Him. God used Esther and Mordecai to rescue people who had not followed His direction. The Jews who remained in exile in the Persian Empire were there by their own choice. Although their ancestors had originally been driven from their homes in Jerusalem to be exiled in what became the Persian Empire, Persia's leaders later permitted the Jews to return to their homeland. God told the people, through Isaiah and Jeremiah, that they should go to Jerusalem. Some did, but the majority did

---

101   Proverbs 13:10 (NIV)

102   Esther 4:16

not. Yet He protected those who stayed from the annihilation that would have occurred at Haman's instigation. Mordecai and Esther were among the disobedient. Nevertheless, they did the right thing when they learned of Haman's actions, and God protected and used them for His purposes.

We will see evidence of God's foresight in circumstances where He is at work. Many say that the point of the book of Esther is to show God's providence. There is plenty of evidence of God's protective hand in events that, from a worldly perspective, might seem like lucky coincidences but obviously were not. These events changed history.

- Esther was selected as queen after Vashti refused to appear at a king's banquet, and Esther was chosen by a process that was not customary.

- When Haman cast lots to determine the month that the attacks on the Jews would commence, God assured that enough time would pass (eleven months) for events to take place that would allow the Jews to be spared. "The lot is cast into the lap, but its every decision is from the Lord." [103]

- The king was willing to see Esther, even though he had not summoned her.

- The king could not sleep, so the reading of Mordecai's king-saving action led to a series of events in which Mordecai was spared and then honored, and Haman was disgraced.

- Esther delayed answering the king's question until after Mordecai was honored.

- The king was not angered to learn that Esther was a Jew.

---

103   Proverbs 16:33

- Haman fell on Esther's sofa just as the king returned from the garden.

A different outcome for any of these events could have meant death to Esther, Mordecai, and all of the Jews in the Persian kingdom. Yet God showed that with Esther's obedience even the most evil of men could not destroy God's chosen people. "Providence" means "foresight;" God's foresight was evident in the story of Esther. And it can be in our work as well, especially if we are "called for such a time as this."

Concluding Thoughts

We are called to be chaplains "for such a time as this." But what is "this time"?

For some, "this time" could be any time of need for an individual, family, or community. Some say "this time" for those who serve our nation as chaplains began on September 11, 2001, when the reality of terrorism came to our land in a devastating way. That is, 9/11 was "the time" when the need for chaplains and their unique contribution in major crises became recognized in a significant way by government and private agencies that are responsible for disaster recovery and relief efforts.

We see that the need for chaplains is multiplying in "this time" of domestic and foreign natural disasters: Katrina, Rita, Ike, Isabel, and other powerful hurricanes; massive wildfires; record-setting killer tornados; unprecedented floods; crippling ice storms; earthquakes; tsunamis; and other similar events. "This time" is also an era of human-caused tragedies such as suicides and mass shootings in schools, businesses, and other settings. And "this time" is also a period of very difficult economic circumstances resulting in hardship to many families and individuals and a growing need for corporate chaplains. All of these occurrences and others represent "this time" of call to service for chaplains.

Our nation needs chaplains who are like the men of Issachar, who understood the times and knew what Israel should do.[104] God asks us to recognize when it is "this time," a time in which we—not someone else—are called to do His work. He asks us to be forward-leaning, moving toward the crisis and not away from it, knowing what to do under His divine guidance.

---

104   1 Chronicles 12:32

Chapter 13

JESUS, THE MODEL CHAPLAIN

"I HAVE COMPASSION FOR THESE people," Jesus said of the crowd that had been with Him for three days with nothing to eat. "I don't want to send them away hungry, because they might faint on the way."

"Where will we get enough loaves of bread?" His disciples wondered.

"How many do you have?" Jesus responded.

It turned out that they had seven loaves, plus a few small fish. That was enough for Jesus. After giving thanks, he broke and passed the food to his disciples, who in turn distributed it to the crowd. The loaves multiplied until the entire gathering—four thousand men, plus women and children—had been fed. And seven baskets were left over.[105]

Jesus served as a chaplain while He was on earth. He ministered to distressed people wherever He found them—in most cases outside the church (synagogue)—and met both physical and spiri-

---

105 Matthew 15:32-8

tual needs. Most of the examples of His chaplain ministry, like the feeding of the four thousand-plus, involved what we call "miracles." And you're probably thinking: "It was easy for Him to do, because He was without sin and had divine powers. I am just a sinful human being. How can I help people the way He did?"

But Jesus didn't do it alone. He prayed to the Father, asking for His intervention. For example, as Jesus stood at Lazarus' tomb, before He commanded Lazarus to come out of the tomb, He prayed, "Father, I thank You that You hear Me. And I know that You hear Me always." Then, to let us know that He was in communication with the Father, Jesus added, in effect, "I said this out loud so that the people standing around will believe that You sent Me."[106] Jesus' high priestly prayer for His followers (John chapter 17; see the Appendix) is an eloquent example of His intervention with the Father on behalf of others.

And Jesus tells us to pray, as we see in the story of the healing of the demon-possessed boy (Mark 9:14-29). In fact, the story shows that prayer may be absolutely essential if we are going to see the result we desire:

> The man had brought his son, possessed by a spirit that made him mute and subject to violent seizures, to Jesus' disciples for healing. But the disciples were unable to cast the demon out, so they brought the man and his son to Jesus. "If you can do anything, take pity on us and help us," the man said. "If you can!" Jesus repeated the man's words. "All things are possible to him who believes." Jesus rebuked the spirit, commanding it to come out of the boy,

---

106 John 11:41,42

and it did. "Why could we not cast it out?" his disciples asked. *"This kind cannot come out by anything but prayer,"*[107] Jesus replied. (italics added)

Christian chaplains have a resource that is not available to non-Christians—access to the Father through prayer. He wants us to use it.

The Model Chaplain at Work

Jesus came to earth to become the perfect sacrifice for our sins. He came to seek and save the spiritually lost. He performed miracles to prove His divinity. Typically, we study His words and actions so that we might understand His purposes, come to know Him, learn how to live our lives, and know how to witness for Him. But Jesus also served as a chaplain, as a number of New Testament stories illustrate. As you read through the following highlights of some of those stories, taking a close look at what He said and did, you will see principles and practices that you can apply in your own ministry.

Feeding five thousand-plus sheep who did not have a shepherd. Mark 6:30-44. Seeing that His disciples needed a break, Jesus said to them, "Let's get away from the crowds to a solitary place, and rest a while." So they traveled by boat across the Sea of Galilee to what they thought would be a secluded spot. But many people who saw them cast off ran around the seashore to the place Jesus had chosen. Seeing them, Jesus felt compassion, because they were like sheep without a shepherd. So He began teaching them.

---

107 Mark 9:29

By this time it was late in the day, and the disciples told Jesus to send the people out to buy food. "You give them something to eat," Jesus said.

"But it would cost 200 denarii to buy food for them," they responded.

Jesus had a plan. "Go find out what the crowd has," Jesus directed.

The disciples did so, and brought back five loaves and two fish. Jesus looked to heaven and blessed the food, and from it there came enough to feed the crowd of 5,000 men in addition to women and children. A dozen full baskets of food were left over.

The need for faith in a storm. Mark 4: 35-41. The fierce wind brought waves crashing over the small boat, filling it with water. But Jesus, who had been asleep in the stern, slept on. So his disciples awoke him. "Don't you care that we are about to die?" they asked.

Jesus quieted the storm and then rebuked the men: "Why are you so timid? Why is it that you have no faith?"

Healing Jarius' daughter, the sick woman, and two blind men. Mark 5:22-43.

Jesus was on his way to the home of Jarius, a synagogue official whose daughter was on the verge of death. A crowd followed Him, and in that crowd was a woman who had been hemorrhaging for twelve years despite having been treated by many physicians. Desperate, and thinking that touching Jesus' garments would heal her, she put her hand on his cloak—and she was healed.

"Who touched me?" Jesus asked. The crowd had been pressing in on Jesus, and many had come in contact with Him. But he looked around to focus on one person, the woman who had touched his cloak believing that she would be healed. "Your faith has made you well," He said to her.

Continuing on to Jarius' house, Jesus overheard people telling Jarius, "Your daughter has died. Why bother the Teacher?"

But Jesus had reassuring words: "Don't be afraid, only believe. The child has not died, but is asleep."

The people scoffed and sneered. Jesus put the scoffers out of the house and took the parents to the girl's room, where He said, "Little girl, I say to you, arise!" And she did.

As He resumed His travels, two blind men followed, seeking His mercy in healing them. Jesus asked, "Do you believe that I am able to do this?"

"Yes, Lord," they said.

He touched their eyes, saying, "Be it done to you according to your faith." And their eyes were opened.[108]

Sabbath healing: the man with the withered hand. Luke 6:6-11. As Jesus taught in the synagogue on the Sabbath, a man with a withered hand sat in the congregation. The scribes and Pharisees watched closely to see if Jesus would heal the man on the Sabbath, which would be against their tradition. Jesus knew that they were looking for a reason to accuse Him of wrongdoing, but told the man to come forward. He asked the doubters, "Is it lawful on the Sabbath to do good, or to do harm, to save a life, or destroy it?" In other words, not to heal would be to destroy life. So Jesus was saying that Sabbath healing is justified. Jesus told the man to stretch out his

---

hand, and it was restored. Angry, the Jewish leaders discussed what they might do to Jesus.

Casting out a hostile spirit. Luke 4:33-6. "What do we have to do with you, Jesus of Nazareth?" the demon-possessed man said to Jesus. "Be quiet and come out of him," Jesus commanded the demon. And the demon left the man without causing harm.

Two-step healing at Bethsaida. Mark 8:22-6. At Bethsaida, the people brought a blind man to Jesus, asking Him to touch the man. Jesus spat on the man's eyes and laid hands on him, then asked, "Do you see anything?"

The man responded, "I see men, like trees, walking around." Then Jesus laid His hands on the man's eyes, the man looked intently, and he began to see everything clearly.

"We tried it before, and it didn't work." Luke 5:1-11. "Put your boat out into deep water and let down your nets for a catch," Jesus told Simon Peter.

Jesus' disciple was not in a receptive mood. He and other fishermen had labored all night, but had not caught anything. Nevertheless, he said, "At Your bidding I will let down the nets." Simon Peter and his partners, James and John, caught enough fish to fill two boats so full of fish that the boats started to sink. "Get away from me, because I am a sinful man," Simon Peter said to Jesus.

"Do not fear," Jesus replied, "from now on you will be catching men."

Turning water to wine, and this wasn't your average wine. John 2:1-11. Jesus had been invited to a wedding, and on the third day the wine jugs were empty. This was a major embarrassment for the bride and groom since it was a serious breach of etiquette to run out of wine during a wedding celebration.

"Fill these water pots with water," Jesus instructed. When this was done, He told them to draw some out and take it to the head-waiter. The headwaiter tasted it and found that it was wine. And it was not ordinary wine. "Every man serves the good wine first," the waiter said to the bridegroom, "but you have kept the good wine until now."

Bringing a widow's son back to life. Luke 7:11-17. As Jesus approached a city gate, He saw a coffin containing the body of a man, the only son of a widow, being carried out of the city. When he saw the widow, he felt compassion and said to her, "Do not weep." He touched the coffin, and the dead man came to life. The large crowd that had accompanied the funeral procession began glorifying God.

"Do you want to get well?" John 5:1-15. There was a pool, called Bethesda, near one of Jerusalem's gates. People who were sick lay under shelters near the pool, waiting for the water to be stirred by an angel so they might be healed when they entered the pool. Jesus came by and saw a man who had been sick for thirty-eight years. Knowing that, Jesus asked the man, "Do you want to get well?" The man answered by saying that he had no one to help him into the pool when the water was stirred. Jesus responded by saying, "Arise, take up your pallet, and walk." And he did.

Who's to blame? John 9:1-7. As Jesus passed a man who had been blind from birth, his disciples asked, "Who sinned, the man or his parents, to cause him to be born blind?"

Neither, He said, but the man was blind "so that the works of God might be displayed in him." Then He added, "We must work the works of Him who sent Me, as long as it is day; night is coming, when no man can work." And Jesus restored the man's sight.

"Neither do I condemn you." John 8:1-11. When the scribes and Pharisees brought a woman caught in adultery to Him, Jesus didn't directly answer the question they asked: Should she be stoned? Instead, He challenged them. "He who is without sin among you, let him cast the first stone." After all the men went away, Jesus said to the woman, "Did no one condemn you?" When she answered "no one," He said, "Neither do I condemn you; go your way, and sin no more."

"Lazarus, come forth!" John 11:1-44. Lazarus, brother of Jesus' friends Mary and Martha, was sick. So the sisters called for Jesus to come to Bethany in Judea, where Lazarus lay ill. He said, "The sickness is not unto death but for the glory of God, that the Son of God may be glorified by it." So He made plans to go to Judea, despite warnings from His disciples that the Jews there were seeking to stone Him. He delayed, and by the time Jesus arrived in Bethany, Lazarus had died and had been in the tomb four days.

Martha went to meet Jesus, lamenting, "If You had been here, my brother would not have died."

Jesus assured her, "Your brother shall rise again." When He saw the mourners, Jesus was deeply moved in His spirit, and was troubled. When they told Jesus to come and see Lazarus' body, He wept.

But some of the Jews said, "Could not this man, who opened the eyes of the blind, have kept this man from dying?"

Jesus asked that the stone be rolled away from the tomb. After He prayed, He commanded, "Lazarus, come forth." Lazarus did so, and Jesus said, "Unbind him[109] and let him go."

Watch and pray. Matthew 26: 36-45. It was Jesus' darkest hour as He entered the Garden of Gethsemane. He asked His disciples to stay and "keep watch with me," while He went a little further to pray. But they were asleep when he came back. Chastising them, He directed that they "watch and pray, lest you enter into temptation." He went to pray again and, on returning again found them asleep "for their eyes were heavy." When the same thing happened a third time, He said, "Are you still sleeping and resting? Behold, the hour is at hand, and the Son of Man is betrayed into the hands of sinners. Rise, let us be going. See, My betrayer is at hand."

Behold your mother! John 19:25-27. As Jesus hung on the cross, He saw His mother standing nearby. His disciple John was there as well. "Woman, behold your son!" He said to her, referring to John. (In other words, John would become like a son to her.) Then, to John He said, "Behold, your mother". (Treat her as if she were your mother). And from that hour, John took Mary into his own household.

Thoughts for the Chaplain

Jesus was the model of compassion. He showed His concern for individuals as well as large groups. He put His compassion into action by feeding people who were hungry, teaching people who were like sheep without a shepherd, and helping a widow whose only son had died. The story of Lazarus shows the depth of His

---

109 Remove the grave clothes.

compassion: Jesus was deeply moved in His spirit, and He wept. He cared enough about another person—the woman with the hemorrhage—to find her in the crowd and speak to her individually. His compassion stirred Him to action when he had other things to do or needed rest.

He delegated responsibility to His chaplains (disciples). He gave the disciples assignments in feeding the two large groups of people. He sent them out in the community to proclaim the kingdom of God, giving them power and authority over all the demons and power to heal diseases.[110] He didn't do it all himself.

He expected His disciples to have faith. For example, He challenged the disciples to have faith when they thought the storm would capsize their boat. And He admonished them not to give up—to have faith in His instruction—when they had not caught any fish during the night. "We have tried it before," was not an acceptable excuse or a worthy substitute for faith.

He taught us much about how to interact with those we serve. As a major theme of His ministry, *He expected faith from those who needed His healing touch.* "All things are possible to him who believes," He told the father of the demon-possessed boy. He had a similar message at Jarius' house, saying "don't be afraid, only believe." And He asked, "Do you believe that I am able to heal you?" of the two blind men. *He made sure that people really wanted His help.* "Do you want to get well?" He asked the man at the Bethesda pool, showing that it is a waste of time to try to help someone who doesn't want to improve his condition. *He did not condemn the woman whose behavior had put her in distress.* He made it clear to the adulterous woman that

---

110   Mark 6:7-13; Luke 9:1-6

He would not condemn her. But He also admonished her not to repeat her behavior. *He helped people offer their best,* as in the case of the Cana couple who ran out of wine. *He moved right ahead with His ministry in the face of hostility*—when the demon-possessed man asked, "What do we have to do with you, Jesus of Nazareth?" Jesus told the demon, essentially, "Shut up and come out of him."

He showed how to deal with detractors and doubters. Jesus addressed the scribes and Pharisees upfront when He knew that they would condemn Him for healing a withered hand on the Sabbath. In doing so, He taught that sometimes issues must be dealt with at the time they arise, even if they are unspoken. "The elephant in the room" —in this case, the issue of healing on the Sabbath—needed to be addressed.

Jesus quieted the doubters and scoffers at Jarius' house by telling them to believe and by pressing on to accomplish His purpose of bringing the daughter back to life. He dealt with "if only" and "it's too late" by reassuring Lazarus' friends and family and then by restoring life to Lazarus' body.

He did not avoid dangerous situations where He was called to minister. He knew that after He healed the man on the Sabbath, the scribes and Pharisees would discuss what to do with Him, possibly planning to harm Him. But He healed the man anyway. He went to Lazarus' home despite warnings that He would be stoned.

He showed that meeting a person's needs may require patience. Jesus first step in healing the blind man at Bethsaida resulted in the man being able to see, but only dimly. Full healing required a second effort on Jesus' part—he zeroed in on the problem area by putting his hands on the man's eyes. (Note also that extra effort was required of the one being helped—the second time, the man looked intently before being able to see clearly).

He dealt gracefully with interruptions and diversions. Jesus and his disciples boated across the sea to rest; they were interrupted by a mass of people who longed for His teaching. He was on His way to Jarius' house when a woman diverted His attention by touching His garments. Jesus' ministry on earth involved a series of interruptions. Each time He responded gracefully, sacrificing His time to meet the need in front of Him before moving on to the next ministry opportunity.

His ministry not only met needs but also resulted in abundance. The gathering of the five thousand-plus had only five loaves and two fish to offer; a dozen full baskets were left after Jesus fed them all. The four thousand-plus offered seven loaves and a few fish, they ate their fill, and yet seven baskets were left. As chaplains, we can ask for God's provision that not only meets but also surpasses the basic needs of the people.

He taught us about the vital need for the "ministry of presence" with one who is distraught. During His time of agony in the Garden of Gethsemane, He called on the disciples to keep watch ("stay awake, be alert"[111]) and pray. This time He did not act as a chaplain but instead called on others to minister to Him by being there. The disciples learned that practicing the ministry of presence is not easy; they fell asleep! "Keeping watch involves active emotional and

---

111   The Ryrie Study Bible, *supra,* footnote to Matthew 26:38. Reprinted by permission of Moody Publications, Chicago IL.

spiritual presence in addition to physical presence."[112] Our inclination is to want to do or say something, but there are times when what's needed is for the chaplain to just be there without trying to fix the problem or offer advice. "When people realize they are not alone in the time of their suffering, the fact that the chaplain has not abandoned them may enable them to believe that God has not abandoned them either."[113]

Jesus cared for others even in His most desperate hour. While He was on the cross, Jesus made provision for His mother's care. This was an act of *compassion* for Mary, of course; it was also a *delegation* to John. When He told John to care for Mary as if she were His mother, He let us know that there are circumstances where a chaplain might treat nonfamily members just as well as the chaplain might care for a family member (though not necessarily bringing them into our household on an indefinite basis). Finally, our model chaplain remembered someone who was in need (His mother) even though He was going through the greatest crisis of His time on earth. Other lessons can be learned from this story. For example, the incident reminds us that we can encourage those who are terminally ill to make adequate provisions for their surviving family members.

God received the glory from His ministry. The people glorified God after Jesus brought the widow's only son back to life. Lazarus' sickness was for the glory of God, Jesus told Mary and Martha. A man had been blind from birth, not because of anyone's sin, but so that "the works of God may be displayed in him." This episode provided

---

112   Paget, Naomi K. and Janet R. McCormack, "The Work of the Chaplain," Judson Press 2006, p. 9. Reprinted with permission.

113   *Id., p. 10.*

Jesus with the opportunity to tell of *the sense of urgency on our work:* *"We must work the works of Him [the Father] who sent Me, as long as it is day; night is coming, when no man can work."*[114]

"It is finished." Jesus' night on earth had come as He hung on the cross. His last words were, "It is finished." He had accomplished what He came to do. It is our high calling to achieve our purposes by serving people through the power of the Holy Spirit (who Jesus sent to those on earth after descending into heaven)—reaching beyond ourselves to achieve an "it is finished" moment. With His help, and using the gifts He has given us, we can accomplish what He asked us to do. This will earn His praise, "Well done, good and faithful servant!"[115]   But that's not all. By serving those in need (for example, the hungry and thirsty, those in need of clothing and shelter, the sick and the imprisoned), we will have served Him.[116]

---

114   John 9:4

115   Matthew 25:21 (NIV)

116   Matthew 25:31–40

PRAYERS FROM CHAPLAINS' HEARTS

Prayers by Pat Geyer

Chaplains often encounter people who have had devastating losses of material things (such as homes and possessions) that the chaplains cannot replace; illnesses they cannot cure; and deaths they cannot reverse. In such cases, the chaplain's service may be that of presence, psychological and spiritual support—and prayer. In any given encounter, prayer may be the most important—and possibly the only—service the chaplain can offer. No matter the circumstance, the chaplain's offer of prayer will rarely be turned down.

We prefer spontaneous, Spirit-driven prayer. Yet, we can learn much about how to pray by reading the prayers of others. We trust that reading these prayers will enrich your own prayer experiences.

Note: Some of the following prayers are e-mail prayers and have been generalized to avoid identification of the people involved; others are examples of the types of prayers Pat offers in face-to-face encounters in her ministry. Two prayers from Scripture are also included.

In Times of Illness

Heavenly Father,

We cry out to you this evening for our precious sister. Father, you are the maker of her soul and body. You know the problem that ails her. We stand together and ask that you bring a healing touch to her body and allow the growths to not only be removed, but to be benign as well. Breathe your breath of comfort and joy into her so she will not be anxious during the wait for the biopsy results. When the doctors decide what to do for her, please give them the mind of Christ. Cause them to be wise and discerning beyond their own ability. Bring the supernatural into her surgery room and her post-surgery recuperation. Guide the surgeon's hands as he removes the unhealthy tissue. Let there be a minimal amount of discomfort and bring her back to wellness as quickly as possible. We depend on you, and you alone Father, to heal her body. Give her husband and kids confidence and comfort also. We give you all the glory and honor and praise as each of us petitions you once again for our dear sister in Christ. Thank you for always hearing our concerns, and we remember what your Word encourages us to do: "Pray without ceasing."

We close our prayer in the glorious name above all names, Jesus. Amen.

Father Above,

Thank you for being with us this day. There are so many times you could turn your eyes from us, but you never do. How is it that with all the sin you see in the world, sin your Son Jesus died for on the cross, you still find us worthy and bend an ear to us? Thank you for that great blessing. Jesus, our Intercessor, You know we are helpless without you and your mighty work of salvation. We all thank you for your act of love on the cross. It is to our great delight that we are able to bask in that forgiveness.

Before the throne of God this day, we place this man and all his medical issues. They may seem perplexing to us, but to you they are a chance for us to see your divine glory from the throne room. Show us how to pray for this man and his wife. Reveal to the doctors how they are to respond to his needs when they review the results of his tests and learn of the treatment he needs for his cancer. It is never easy for us to see anyone struggle in the physical. Lord, only you can provide healing for him. Give relief to each and every cell in his body. Wrap your healing grace around him with pure water from the living well of Jesus. Living water that refreshes the spirit and the flesh. Carry antibodies of grace and blessings to his innermost being, causing a well of great joy and delight to come into his entire body for healing. May the assurance of the living Word of God spring forth in him to bring about a strong mind, body and spirit. Make all things new, and may they work together for the good of the gospel. Give him again a powerful testimony from Jesus to spread across the country and around the world.

Carry his wife in your arms of tender love as she cares for him. Strengthen her heart, spirit, mind, and entire body. Allow her to help by strengthening her own heart for you and her physical body. Give delight and blessing to her with each word of this prayer so she can proclaim that you and you alone once again extended great mercy to both her and her husband. Encourage both of them in ways we cannot. If you made provision for your own mother while you were dying on the painful cross, surely you will care for this dear couple in their hour of need. Thank you for showing all of us your kindness and compassion.

As a family of believers, we cry out to you in one accord and carry this prayer for healing to you. You designed people to be a support for one another, so we are claiming that support as you answer our prayer, Lord.

In the beautiful and precious name of Jesus, amen.

In Times of Death

Heavenly Father,

We are as broken as one can be over the sad loss of this man. We ask that you give an extra amount of grace to his family. Bless his wife with your strength; make her strong and able to withstand the sorrow she must walk through. Give her happy memories of her dear husband and allow her to find comfort in you, Lord, and also her child. Spare any extra grief or harm to this family and build up their strength so what they are going through will draw them to you if they don't already know you, Lord. We don't want one person to be lost and not belong to you before they leave this world. Use this event to draw them to your heart. We cry out for their souls and claim them as yours, knowing and believing you have heard our cry.

We pray you will empower this man's friends and acquaintances with wisdom and discernment in a supernatural way. You tell us in the Word if we ask for it, you will give it to us, so we are asking. Comfort their hearts so they can heal.

We can't understand the reason for this man's death, but we can know that You love his family and friends more than they know. Your Son proved that on the cross, so we cling to the promise of His sacrifice. That gives us all hope for each new day. Numb the aching hearts. It is hard to see them go through this trial.

Thank you for hearing our prayer. Hold everyone close to you and protect them until this storm passes. We will continue to praise you no matter what the circumstances. Amen, dear Jesus.

Loss of House and Possessions

Father,

You are a God of renewal and restoration who hears our prayers during times of need. Thank you for being merciful and allowing us to express our pain for this dear family. A great burden of loss has come into their lives, and we are here to hopefully lift some of that burden by praying for them. They are our brothers and sisters, and when they hurt, we hurt. Although we cannot begin to know how they feel, we do know they need our love and support. Enable us to bring to them some relief or assistance in whatever small way we can. Thank you for each family member who was protected from serious personal harm during this storm and for allowing each person to hold fast to the beautiful memories from their destroyed home. No storm can steal those memories from them. May those memories be like a treasure to them and help them find creative ways to record them so their future generations will have them to hold on to.

Allow us to hear and understand their emotional, spiritual, and day-to-day needs so we can walk with them and be a stabilizing force through you for them.

You tell us to love one another, and we are here for that purpose. We pray you will give these dear people strength that comes directly from you and that when they are most weary, they will feel in their spirit your gentle hand of love covering them.

Finally, Father, remind them of this prayer that we prayed for them today, and bring to them the trust in you they will need to help them move through the days ahead. May they have a desire to meet with you in prayer, individually and as a family, because ultimately you are the one who will bring to their hearts a peace that will surpass all human understanding. Thank you for hearing our prayer. We offer this prayer knowing that your divine love will sustain these people because you are a God who answers prayer. Amen.

Prayer for One Who is Seeking God

I stand before you, God, acknowledging that I know you, but that this dear man I'm praying with isn't sure about who you are and what place you may have in his life. It seems that man's words can only go so far, and then we are left with a void and a silence that at times like this can be deafening. I know there is something more to life than just going through trials leaning on one's own self.

I'm asking, God, that you show yourself to him just as you did to me. Allow him to trust that there is no harm in seeking you out in prayer and just reading the Bible. There is no agenda on my part to have this man join a particular church or denomination. I only want him to find that place of peace that comes from knowing who you are and what you have already done for him in his life. Help him to know you and encourage him in quiet times to just talk with you in truth, no matter what is on his heart. That is all prayer is: an ordinary conversation with an extraordinary God. That is why prayer fills our hearts with peace, and then you reveal yourself to us at your chosen time.

That is what I'm asking for in this prayer: an opportunity for this man to seek you out in private or with another person, and for you to help him desire to discover you in the Bible without thinking about any agenda on anyone's part. Fill the need he has to be connected to more than this world in which he lives. Give him the gift of faith in Jesus that will carry him to the end of his life on earth and then into heaven, where he can spend eternity with you.

I thank you for hearing my prayer, and with joy I rest in the knowledge that this man will come to know your everlasting love. Amen.

Prayer for a Member of the Armed Services

Father,

We pray that your guiding hand will continue to be over this one, and we give you praise and thank you for his safety. It is counted as a high honor for him to serve both you and his country. Give extra grace and blessings to him this day and hold him close to your side while he serves his nation. Rest his body, mind, and spirit with your peace and love. Draw his family and friends close to him. We look forward to a time of shared friendship with him.

Praise and honor and glory to you, Abba Father. Amen.

Prayer for First Responders

Lord,

I place these first responders before you and ask that you protect them from the dangers they encounter every day. They are gallant men and women who have chosen to help those in need in circumstances from which most of us would run. May each one of them belong to you in a personal way. Make them steadfast in courage and strong in body and mind and spirit. Instill in them a supernatural ability to know you are with them and to know when you want them to go forward and when you want them to retreat. When they rush to save lives, bless them and protect them from harm's way. Shower your love on them because they are so unselfish and are willing to serve people with their very own lives at stake. That is so familiar to Christians because we know Jesus did that very thing. He gave his life for us. We give these people honor for being like you, Jesus.

Truly, we are not all called to stand in the presence of such danger as these brave first responders, but we are all called to pray for them. Remind us often to pray with fervent hearts that they will call out for your divine love and protection to be poured over them because you are their great Protector. Give their leaders the wisdom to know what is best for them when they are in the line of duty and when there is a need for compassion and rest. Keep all team members together when there is danger and allow them to work in unity with one purpose in mind, to complete the task at hand without injury and without confusion. We ask this because you are a God of order in all situations. Help their work be timely and end with positive results. Especially, Lord, give them resilient minds that are able to process the events they see while working, and strengthen their emotional coping abilities for those events.

At the end of the day, bring rest and restoration to their minds and bodies and allow them to find pleasure in their families and other healthy outlets. Protect their marriages and bless their children. We ask that their spouses and children not be overcome by fear because of the dangerous work they are involved in. Always have a listening ear for each responder when they need to talk. May this chaplain's prayer be a reminder to them that the Lord knows all their needs and is with them whenever they serve Him or people in need. Again, I thank you for these courageous men and women who serve you and their communities every day.

I now rest my prayer in your throne room, knowing you have heard and answered my requests. Amen.

Prayer for Chaplain Leaders

Heavenly Father,

This is a new day and a new opportunity for us to worship and honor you. I find great pleasure in that. As the year moves ahead, I ask a special blessing for all of the leaders who so faithfully serve you while building an army of chaplains. We live in a time that so needs the help and work of the chaplaincy. Your word, Father, in 1 Timothy 1:12 says that you have counted us faithful and that you enable us to do ministry. In all the power of heaven I lay claim to that verse for chaplain leaders, and all the present and future chaplains. Thank you for giving us that confidence and that Word.

I ask that you guard the spiritual, physical, and emotional lives of our leaders. Protect them and keep unity throughout the organization by the power of your grace. Give them an extra portion of wisdom, discernment, strength, and encouragement. As they move forward, bind all future attempted attacks that are meant to cause harm in any way. It is the Word of God that gives me the authority of this prayer, and I claim that authority right now.

Looking back I remember when one of our leaders said not to let anyone discourage us or take from us our plans and desires for serving You in the future. I ask that you not let anyone do that to our leaders. Cause people to edify the chaplain cause and build up our leaders so they will have strength to carry out their intense schedules. Bless them in every way. Shower grace and blessings on them and their dear families. Bring a unity and healing in all areas of need in their lives so that they can serve you with joy and great pleasure. Remind them often that they are a great inspiration to those of us who also follow hard after you. Finally, may we all feel the arms of unity and love in our lives, knowing that unity comes directly from you.

Thank you, Abba Father, for the privilege of this prayer for our leaders, and for bending your ear low to hear my heart's desires. Amen, Jesus!

Prayer for Fellow Chaplains

I praise you, heavenly Father, for this is a new day that you have made, and I shall rejoice in it just as your Word tells me to do. You are the very breath of life. In humility I ask that you forgive me of any sins that I have committed so I can come to you as a little child dependent upon my Father's love. I choose to enter your holy throne room in humility and under your covering of grace while I present to you my request for the men and women you have called to be an army of chaplains. I desire to be pleasing to you while I bow down and lay my petitions before you. There is no better place for them or me than in the grip of your divine love and protection.

Father, I pray for the precious chaplains you have called to serve you "for such a time as this." Cause the Holy Spirit to awaken in them your soft voice of instruction that will always lead them in power and authority from above. May the Word of God be their armor during all times of ministry so that "no weapon formed against them shall prosper." Let no misconceptions or distractions from the enemy come before them. The enemy would love to devour and destroy the work that you, Father, have laid out before each one of them. I seek your divine protection for them against the spirit of darkness. In the name of Jesus, under the covering of the blood of the cross, I rebuke the evil plans of Satan. If you are with the chaplains, who can be against them? By the power of the supernatural, keep them from harm's way in the spiritual, physical, and emotional areas of their lives. Keep them of strong mind and body so they can serve you as long as your breath of life is in them.

Strengthen and protect their families so that when they serve you and the many needs of hurting people, they can serve without distraction but with both confidence and assurance, knowing you are in control of all things in their life. Teach each one to know when to rest and when to serve. Set clear boundaries before them so they serve only in the areas you have chosen for them and not in areas their flesh might think of. I know your financial provision will always be at hand for them when they are called to serve the Father, and I thank you in advance for that comfort.

Bring joy every morning to your army of chaplains so that they serve you with delight in their hearts in ways that always bring honor to you in all things at all times. Keep them aware of your supernatural works. Make humility part of the armor of God they wear daily so the forces of darkness will not be able to mislead them into thinking man can do the supernatural works of God. Protect their minds from spiritual deception and give them "the mind of Christ, lest they should boast of any man's works." Cause them to follow hard after you while continuing to grow in Christ by leaning on and learning the Word of God. Please destroy any deceptions of the world that would impair their service to you, dear Lord.

Finally, Father, I ask that you keep a clear vision before each chaplain so they can recognize your planned will for them every day of their lives. Amen.

Nehemiah's Prayer for a Nation

When I heard these things [destruction of Jerusalem's wall], I sat down and wept. For some days I mourned and fasted and prayed before the God of heaven. Then I said:

"O LORD, God of heaven, the great and awesome God, who keeps his covenant of love with those who love him and obey his commands, let your ear be attentive and your eyes open to hear the prayer your servant is praying before you day and night for your servants, the people of Israel. I confess the sins we Israelites, including myself and my father's house, have committed against you. We have acted very wickedly toward you. We have not obeyed the commands, decrees and laws you gave your servant Moses.

"Remember the instruction you gave your servant Moses, saying, 'If you are unfaithful, I will scatter you among the nations, but if you return to me and obey my commands, then even if your exiled people are at the farthest horizon, I will gather them from there and bring them to the place I have chosen as a dwelling for my Name.'

"They are your servants and your people, whom you redeemed by your great strength and your mighty hand. O Lord, let your ear be attentive to the prayer of this your servant and to the prayer of your servants who delight in revering your name. Give your servant success today by granting him favor in the presence of this man."

Nehemiah 1:4-11 (New International Version, NIV)

Jesus' High Priestly Prayer

A Prayer for Unity, Protection, Holiness, Witness, and Glorification of Those Who Would Form His Church

Note: This is an excellent source of inspiration for prayer for our fellow chaplains and others with whom we work—and for ourselves.

"My prayer is not for the world, but for those you have given me, because they belong to you. All who are mine belong to you, and you have given them to me, so they bring me glory. Now I am departing from the world; they are staying in this world, but I am coming to you. Holy Father, you have given me your name; now protect them by the power of your name so that they will be united just as we are. During my time here, I protected them by the power of the name you gave me. I guarded them so that not one was lost, except the one headed for destruction, as the Scriptures foretold.

"Now I am coming to you. I told them many things while I was with them in this world so they would be filled with my joy. I have given them your word. And the world hates them because they do not belong to the world, just as I do not belong to the world. I'm not asking you to take them out of the world, but to keep them safe from the evil one. They do not belong to this world any more than I do. Make them holy by your truth; teach them your word, which is truth. Just as you sent me into the world, I am sending them into the world. And I give myself as a holy sacrifice for them so they can be made holy by your truth.

"I am praying not only for these disciples but also for all who will ever believe in me through their message. I pray that they will all be one, just as you and I are one—as you are in me, Father, and I am in you. And may they be in us so that the world will believe you sent me.

"I have given them the glory you gave me, so they may be one as we are one. I am in them and you are in me. *May they experience such perfect unity that the world will know that you sent me and that you love them as much as you love me. Father, I want these whom you have given me to be with me where I am. Then they can see all the glory you gave me because you loved me even before the world began!*

"O righteous Father, the world doesn't know you, but I do; and these disciples know you sent me. I have revealed you to them, and I will continue to do so. Then your love for me will be in them, and I will be in them."

John 17:9-26 (New Living Translation) (italics added)

GUIDE FOR BIBLE STUDY

Chapter 1 – The Heart of a Chaplain: Who is a Chaplain's Neighbor?

IMAGINE A SCENARIO WHERE YOU see someone in distress, e.g., a person or family stopped by the side of the road with car trouble, someone in a mall who appears to be ill, or a person in a hospital waiting room who is distraught. Would you try to help? What if it seems that you might be in danger or treated rudely if you intervened? What if you had an important appointment to keep? How might you help even if you are not in a position to minister directly to the person?

Have you had experiences similar to those just described? What did you do?

Read the story of the Good Samaritan (Luke 10:25-37).

Who is our neighbor—one that we should love as ourselves—according to the story?

In verses 31 and 32, what might the priest and Levite have been thinking when they saw the man? What was their concept of "neighbor"?

What character trait caused the Good Samaritan to help the man? See verse 33.

What reasons (excuses) might the Good Samaritan have had to pass on without helping?

In what ways did the Good Samaritan give of what he had, both tangible and intangible? See verses 34-5.

How did the Good Samaritan prove to be a neighbor? See verses 36-7.

Did the Good Samaritan act as a chaplain? Why or why not? Does it matter that (as far as we know) he didn't minister to the man's spiritual needs? See the definition of "chaplain" in the preface to this book.

Can only those who have the spiritual gift of mercy (compassion) serve as chaplains? Why or why not?

What have you learned (or have had reinforced) from the study of this story, i.e., what are your personal "take home" points?

Chapter 2 – Ministering to the Enemy: Ananias Serving Saul

Read Acts 9:1-31, 22:1-16.

You sense that God is asking you to help someone, and the need is immediate. You are busy on an important project. What do you say to God? Does it make a difference if the important project is for your church?

What did Ananias say when God called him? See Acts 9:10. What did Ananias mean when he said "Here am I, Lord"?

Have you had a call from God similar to His assignment to Ananias? How did you respond? Was it like Ananias' reaction? Or was it more like that of Jonah? See Jonah 1:3.

You learn that the person you are to help has been extremely hostile toward Christians. Will that influence your decision to help? Is it okay to be afraid and to tell God of your fears? See Acts 9: 13-14. What if you have learned that the individual has been chosen by God to serve Him? See Acts 9:15-16. What did Ananias do after his conversation with the Lord? See Act 9:17.

How did Ananias minister to Saul? See Acts 9:17-19 and
Acts 22: 12-16. List the various ways in which Ananias
ministered to Saul.

Could God have restored Saul's sight without getting
Ananias involved? Why did he choose a man to intervene? What were Ananias' qualifications to do what
God asked? See Acts 22: 12, but also see Acts 9:10 and
9:17.

Was Ananias acting as a chaplain in this story? Why or why
not? What traits did Ananias exhibit that are important
to chaplains?

What have you learned (or have had reinforced) from the
study of this story, i.e., what are your personal "take
home" points?

Chapter 3 – Shipwrecked: Ministering in a Storm

Read Acts 27:1 through Acts 28:15.

What did Paul rely on when he warned the ship's leaders about the dangers of continuing to travel beyond Fair Haven? That is, how was he able to perceive that trouble was ahead? See Acts 27: 9-10.

What status or authority did Paul have to give advice to the ship's leaders when the ship was in Fair Haven? Would you have spoken up in a similar situation?

What was the state of mind of those who were on the ship as they sailed in the fierce storm without direction? See Acts 27:20. What can chaplains such as Paul offer to people in similar circumstances?

Read Paul's message to his shipmates in Acts 27: 21-26. In view of their earlier rejection of Paul's advice, what might Paul have done or said at this point instead of what he did do and say? How would you have reacted if you were in a similar situation?

What was the essence of Paul's message that would have been helpful to the others on the ship, i.e., what was he trying to convey when he told them to keep up their courage? (Hint: it's a four-letter word).

What practical advice did Paul give to those on the ship? What witness for the Lord did he give, and what were the results? See Acts 27: 33-38, and also verses 21 through 26.

What did the support of fellow Christians do for Paul? See Acts 28:14-15.

Was Paul acting as a chaplain in this story? Why or why not? What traits did Paul exhibit that are important to chaplains, especially those who minister during or immediately after a natural disaster?

What have you learned (or have had reinforced) from the study of this story, i.e., what are your personal "take home" points?

Chapter 4 – Risking Your Life to Help a Fellow Christian

A FELLOW CHRISTIAN—PERHAPS A MISSIONARY OR chaplain that your church supports—is in need. You have been asked to go to that person, who lives in a remote place, to provide assistance. The travel will be grueling and, once there, you will be asked to work long hours to help this person. If you go, what benefits might result for you and others? How do you decide whether to make the trip?

Read Philippians 2:19-30 and 4:10-19.

From the church's perspective, what was Epaphroditus' mission? See Philippians 2:25, 4:18.

What else did Epaphroditus' mission turn out to be? See Philippians 2:25. (Epaphroditus was also a messenger from Paul to the Philippians, having brought Paul's letter to the Philippians back with him.)

How did the Philippian church benefit from having collected and sent the gift with Epaphroditus? See Philippians 4:17-19, 2 Corinthians 8:1-5.

How did Epaphroditus sacrifice? How much should a chaplain risk in serving others?

Suppose you were in Paul's situation. You have acted as a chaplain but now are being served by another. How would you respond? Would it be as Paul responded?

Was the money the point of the story? If not, why not?

Was Epaphroditus acting as a chaplain in this story? Why or why not? What traits did Epaphroditus exhibit that are important to chaplains?

What have you learned (or have had reinforced) from the study of this story, i.e., what are your personal "take home" points?

Chapter 5 – Creativity in Ministering to Others

Read Mark 2:1-12.

Besides doing what they did, what else might the men have done when they saw that their path to Jesus was blocked by the crowd? Consider actions that would have been either positive or negative from the paralyzed man's viewpoint.

Can you share a story in which you or someone else was creative in getting assistance for a person in need?

Jesus healed the man because of faith. Whose faith? Faith in what or whom? See verse 5.

Jesus encountered detractors as he went about healing the man. Although the story doesn't tell us so, the four men also might have run into opposition. What kinds of objections might others have raised to what the men did? How could the men have dealt with such objections? (Consider how Jesus responded to his detractors; see Chapter 13 of this book.)

What obstacles have you encountered as you helped others? How did you respond?

Jesus ministered to the paralyzed man's spiritual needs before taking care of his physical problem. Which needs should come first—the spiritual or the physical? Explain your answer.

What effects did the experience have on others who were present? Who received the glory?

Were the four men acting as chaplains in this story? Why or why not? What traits did the men exhibit that are important to chaplains?

What have you learned (or have had reinforced) from the study of this story, i.e., what are your personal "take home" points?

Chapter 6 – What Shall I Do?
What a Little Jar of Oil and
a Lot of Faith Can Do

Read 2 Kings 4:1-7.

Apparently, Elisha knew the widow's late husband. Should personal acquaintance make a difference in a decision whether to help someone? Consider the Bible's commands to care for widows (for example, Psalms 68:5 and 146:9, Isaiah 1:17, and James 1:27).

Why did Elisha ask the question, "What shall I do for you?" Did he mean that he might solve the problem for her? Was he asking permission to offer assistance to her? Or could he have had something else in mind?

What is the significance of Elisha's answering his own question by asking the woman what she had in her house, and by telling her to ask to borrow vessels from her neighbors? How would the woman benefit by contributing to the solution?

What is the significance of Elisha's telling her to "not get a few" vessels from the neighbors?

What were the benefits of Elisha's giving specific instruction to the widow (verse 4)?

What did Elisha do after giving directions to the woman?

Verse 7 tells us there was more than enough oil to pay the debt. Was the extra amount (enough for the woman and her sons to live on) part of the woman's original goal? Was it part of Elisha's original goal?

What parts of the story describe faith on the woman's part? On Elisha's part?

Was Elisha acting as a chaplain in this story? Why or why not? What traits did he exhibit that are important to chaplains?

What have you learned (or have had reinforced) from the study of this story, i.e., what are your personal "take home" points?

Chapter 7 – Ministering in a Natural Disaster

Read 1 Kings 17:1-24.

When Elijah asked for the last of the widow's bread (verses 11, 12), who was he putting first? When, if ever, should chaplains put their needs above the needs of the people they are serving?

When did Elijah act in faith in this story? How was his faith tested, and how did he respond?

How did Elijah's actions and his witness for the God of Israel encourage the woman's faith in Elijah's God? How did his prayer that led to her son's recovery affect her faith? See especially verses 14, 15, and 24.

Even though Elijah's faith kept the woman and her son from starvation, she rejected and blamed him when her son died. See verse 18. Have you had a similar experience involving someone you have helped? How did you respond? How did Elijah respond to the woman's outburst?

What did Elijah do after he expressed his own frustration to God? See verses 20 and 21. What is the significance of Elijah's having stretched himself out on the boy three

times? Was it a ritual, or did it mean that Elijah was
persistent in his prayer? Or something else?

Elijah was a prophet to whom God gave responsibility concerning Israel's fate. He was an Israelite who God sent
to be cared for by a Gentile woman—and to rescue her
and her son from starvation. Elijah might have been
uncomfortable in Gentile country and thought that the
assignment—ministering to just two people—was be-
neath his status. Yet he seemed not to object. If not,
why not? Have you been in similar circumstances? If
so, how did you respond?

Was Elijah acting as a chaplain in this story? Why or why
not? What traits did Elijah exhibit that are important to
chaplains? What aspects of the story illustrated the importance of being flexible regarding whom we serve?

What have you learned (or have had reinforced) from the
study of this story, i.e., what are your personal "take
home" points?

Chapter 8 – Ministering to a People at War

Read Exodus 17: 8-16.

Moses was called to help people who had been grumbling and complaining about his leadership. Have you been in a position to minister to someone who had said negative things to you or about you? If so, did you help them?

What did Moses say in verse 9 that indicated he would serve as a chaplain during the battle?

Moses encouraged Israel's soldiers merely by his presence; he did not say a word to them. Have you been in a situation where you have provided the "ministry of presence," i.e., you encouraged someone merely by being there? Or has someone encouraged you just by their presence?

When Moses held up the staff of God, it symbolized prayer for the troops, and Israel's army prevailed. When he let his hands down, the Amalekites had the advantage. What does this tell us about an important characteristic of prayer when chaplains are with people who are in the midst of a difficult struggle? See 1 Thessalonians 5:17. What does this story tell us about the importance of the

chaplain having the "ministry of presence" tool in his
or her chaplain tool belt?

Aaron and Hur helped Moses keep the staff of God held
high. Have you been in situations where you were
helping someone in distress and others came to support
you when you grew tired? Have you served in the support role?

This story involves prayer, presence, and support for the
chaplain from others. If any of these elements had been
missing, would Israel have won the battle? What does
this tell you about the chaplain's need to plan carefully?

The battle was over, the victory was won, but what else
did Moses have to do? See verses 14-16. What things
might today's chaplain have to do after the immediate
problem has been dealt with?

After the battle was over, God promised to continue the
fight against the Amalekites. What does this tell you
about the importance of winning the first battle, i.e.,
overcoming the first obstacle you encounter when you
help someone?

Was Moses acting as a chaplain in this story? Why or why
not? What traits did Moses exhibit that are important
to chaplains?

What have you learned (or have had reinforced) from the study of this story, i.e., what are your personal "take home" points?

Chapter 9 – Saving a Suicidal Man in an Earthquake

Read Acts 16:16-40.

Standing up for God got Paul and Silas in trouble. See Acts
    16: 16-24.   Has this ever happened to you, especially
    when you were trying to help someone? What was the
    end result? Are there circumstances under which it is
    better to keep quiet rather than defend God?

Despite being in prison and in stocks, Paul and Silas prayed
    and sang hymns. What positive results came from this?
    See Acts 16:25. What does the Bible tell us about when
    to rejoice? See Philippians 4:4.

Paul stopped the jailer from killing himself, even though he
    and Silas might have escaped if the jailer had done so.
    See Acts 16: 26-28. Have you been in a situation where
    you knew that helping someone else could put you at a
    disadvantage? What did you do?

What positives resulted from Paul's decision to talk the jailer
    out of suicide? See Acts 16: 29-34.

What would you do or say if someone you were assisting
    said, "tell me about salvation"?

Paul and Silas were released by the magistrates. See Acts 16: 35-40. What does this tell us about the wisdom of Paul's decision to help save the jailer's life? Suppose the two would not have been released—would it have been better for them to let the jailer kill himself so they could escape?

Paul and his coworkers had intended to go somewhere other than Philippi, but God directed them to the city where they not only were sent to prison but also had an opportunity to lead a man and his family to the Lord. See Acts 16: 6-12. Have you been in situations where God redirected you, and as a result you had an opportunity to help others?

What was the benefit of having two chaplains (Paul and Silas) serving together in this episode?

Were Paul and Silas acting as chaplains in this story? Why or why not? What traits did they exhibit that are important to chaplains?

What have you learned (or have had reinforced) from the study of this story, i.e., what are your personal "take home" points?

Chapter 10 – Protecting David

How did Jonathan minister to David's physical, emotional, and spiritual well-being? See 1 Samuel 20:1-11, 20:35-42.

Jonathan risked his life to help David. See 1 Samuel 20:24-34. When, if ever, should a chaplain risk his life to protect another?

Do you approve of the following methods Jonathan used to protect David from the king? Why or why not? Does it matter that Saul was afflicted by an evil spirit?

Disobeying the king's (his father's) orders to kill David. See 1 Samuel 19:1-3.

Helping David to hide. See 1 Samuel 20:12-23.

Lying to Saul about David's whereabouts. See 1 Samuel 20: 1-11, 27-29.

In what way was Jonathan an advocate for David before the king? Was Jonathan's approach subtle or direct? See 1 Samuel 19:4-6. Under what circumstances is advocacy on the part of a distressed person a proper role for a chaplain?

Do you approve of Michal's deception with regard to David's whereabouts? Why or why not? See 1 Samuel 19:11-17. Would it make a difference if Michal had not been related either to David or Saul?

Should Samuel, as a man of God, have helped hide David? How did God intervene for David's benefit? See 1 Samuel 19:18-24.

What did Ahimelech do that would justify his breaking the rule about the holy bread that he gave David to eat? See 1 Samuel 22:13, 15. Would he have been justified in giving the bread if he had not done what he did?

Were Jonathan, Michal, Samuel, and Ahimelech acting as chaplains in this story? Why or why not? What traits did they exhibit that are important to chaplains?

What have you learned (or have had reinforced) from the study of this story, i.e., what are your personal "take home" points?

Chapter 11 – Solving a Major Problem in the Face of Major Opposition

Read Nehemiah 2: 11-16.

What was Nehemiah's first step when he arrived in Jerusalem, and why was that step important to the rebuilding of the wall?

What precautions did Nehemiah take as he made that first step, and why were the safety measures necessary? Do chaplains sometimes need to take similar precautions?

What information did Nehemiah provide to encourage the people to rebuild the wall? See Nehemiah 2:17, 18.

How did Nehemiah respond to the enemy's efforts stop the project in each of the following situations?

When Nehemiah and the people were accused of rebelling against the king. See Nehemiah 2:19-20.

When the enemy's leaders ridiculed the people. See Nehemiah 4:1-6.

When the enemy threatened to attack. See Nehemiah 4:7-14.

When the enemy attempted to lure him to a meeting (Nehemiah 6:1-9) and into the temple (6:10-14).

Have you encountered opposition similar to any of the opposition Nehemiah faced when you have tried to help another person? How did you act in response to the resistance? If you have not had similar experiences, how do you think you would react in such situations?

How did Nehemiah respond when he learned of the internal problems, i.e., Jews taking financial advantage of other Jews? See Nehemiah 5:1-13.

Was Nehemiah acting as a chaplain in this story? Why or why not? What traits did Nehemiah exhibit that are important to chaplains?

What have you learned (or have had reinforced) from the study of this story, i.e., what are your personal "take home" points?

Chapter 12 – A Life or Death Decision "For Such a Time as This"

What did Esther do when she learned of the plan to kill the Jews?   See Esther 4:4-5.   What would you do if you learned that people you know are in danger of being injured or killed?

What risk would Esther encounter if she went to the king to intervene on behalf of her people?   See Esther 4:11. What risks have you encountered as you went about helping others?

Esther responded positively to Mordecai's plea that she might have attained royalty "for such a time as this." Has God placed you in a position in the past where it seemed that He had a "for such a time as this" mission for you to help others? Are you in such a position now?

What was the first thing that Esther did after she decided to see the king? See Esther 4:16.

In going to the king, Esther was making a request of a governmental leader. Are there times when a chaplain might make a similar intervention, e.g., approach a governmental leader with a request on behalf of someone in distress? Can you list some examples?

How was God's providence shown in the circumstances
that led up to the saving of Esther and her people? Have
you seen God's hand during times that you have helped
others?

Was Esther acting as a chaplain in this story? Why or why
not? What traits did Esther exhibit that are important
to chaplains?

What have you learned (or have had reinforced) from the
study of this story, i.e., what are your personal "take
home" points?

Chapter 13 —Jesus, the Model Chaplain

Are you intimidated by the thought of following Jesus' examples in ministering to others? Why or why not? What did Jesus say in Mark 9:29 and do in John 11:41, 42 that makes it believable that we could follow His lead?

Without referring back to chapter 13 in this book, how many of Jesus' character traits that were visible in his ministry can you list? Now go back through the chapter and list those that you missed. Which do you consider to be most important? Which is most frequently mentioned? Which of those traits do you believe that you have?

What does it mean to have compassion for another? Do you recall a time when you had compassion for someone who was in distress? Did the compassion move you to action?

Notice how many times the words "faith" and "believe" appear in chapter 13. Jesus expected his disciples to have faith when they were serving as chaplains. Can you think of circumstances where it was clear that your faith in His power helped bring relief to someone who was suffering?

Jesus also expected those who needed healing to have faith. Can you think of circumstances where it was clear that the faith of someone in distress helped bring relief to that person? How do you approach the issue of faith with someone who needs help but is not a believer?

Jesus explained why healing on the Sabbath is justified. Is it okay for a Christian chaplain to do his or her chaplain work on Sundays? Are there any days or circumstances during which chaplain work would not be appropriate?

Several stories in this chapter illustrate the importance of persistence. Can you think of examples in which your persistence paid off in helping someone in need?

Jesus sometimes said to the sick or those around them "do not be afraid" or "do not weep." What was Jesus' message when He used those words? Would you ordinarily use such words in dealing with the needy and their families and friends? In what other ways could you get across Jesus' message?

Have you encountered people in misery who didn't seem to want to better their situations? If so, why do you believe they did not want to get out of their situations? How have you dealt with them?

Do you feel a sense of urgency in better preparing yourself to be one who ministers outside the church? Why or why not?

What have you learned (or have had reinforced) from this chapter, i.e., what are your personal "take home" points?

ABOUT THE AUTHORS

PAT GEYER IS A SENIOR chaplain ordained by the International Fellowship of Chaplains (IFOC) and is certified by the IFOC as a trainer. She has received the Certificate of Specialized Training in Spiritual Care in Crisis Intervention and the Certificate of Specialized Training in Emergency Services from the International Critical Incident Stress Foundation (ICISF). She is a member of both IFOC and ICISF. She is the Crisis Intervention Specialist for the Carroll County, Maryland Sheriff's Office. The National Sheriffs' Association awarded Pat the 2012 Medal of Merit for her valuable contributions to the field of criminal justice and law enforcement. Since volunteering following Hurricane Katrina (that's where God called her into the chaplaincy), Pat has served as a chaplain at a number of disaster sites across the country and in Haiti. She is a chaplain with Billy Graham Evangelical Association's Rapid Response Team. She has received extensive Federal Emergency Management Agency training and certification, training in suicide prevention and intervention, first aid training, and additional training in other areas related to chaplain work. Pat is a speaker for emergency service agencies and private organizations, encouraging and educating those who serve others in need, are victims of traumatic experiences, or are interested in volunteering. She was recognized as Volunteer of the Year by the Red Cross Blood Program for her county in 2009. Pat is fluent in American Sign Language and has served as a deaf ministry leader within the church. She was the owner of an image consulting business, and a hair and cosmetic salon, retiring after 23 years of work in those fields.

DICK GEYER IS A WRITER, teacher, attorney, former government executive, retired military officer, pioneer, gardener to the community— and a chaplain. He is a senior chaplain ordained by the International Fellowship of Chaplains and devotes his chaplain services to veterans. He authored *When America Turned To God: Spiritual Lessons for our Nation from the Gulf War* (HisLink Communications, 2000), a book that was endorsed by the late Dr. D. James Kennedy and included by The Family Research Council and Coral Ridge Ministries among their featured publications. He has taught Bible studies in three churches and, along with Pat, has led innovative studies that tested the concepts presented in *Chaplains of the Bible*. For several years he and Pat led the prayer ministry in their church, and Dick directed a four-year study in the practice and power of prayer—the foundational tool for the chaplain's toolbox.

Dick had a career as an attorney and manager in a major federal government agency. Also, he had a parallel career as an Army Reserve officer, reaching the rank of colonel as a judge advocate and earning the Bronze Star for Meritorious Service in Kuwait during the first Gulf War. In his retirement, he has served veterans in several ways, including helping a number of them obtain benefits from the Department of Veterans Affairs. A member of the Maryland

Defense Force, he is certified as a Military Emergency Management Specialist.

Shortly after retiring, Dick discovered four and one-half acres of unclaimed land nearly adjacent to the property he and Pat owned. Extensive research led to the Maryland Governor's awarding of a land patent (original land grant) similar to the land grants issued to the pioneers who settled Maryland beginning in the seventeenth century. Each spring on another part of their land, Dick plants an extensive vegetable garden that is not only a place for him to be alone with God but also yields hundreds of pounds of fresh vegetables. Dick shares the produce—through his "First Fruits" ministry—with low-income families and individuals, and senior residents in the local community.

DICK AND PAT HAVE FOUR children, seven grandchildren and three rescued cats. They live on sixteen tranquil acres in Maryland that include eleven-plus acres called "Fellowship Forest" in addition to "Lost Acres," the patented property.

For more information about
Richard & Patricia Geyer
&

Chaplains of the Bible
please visit:

www.chaplainsofthebible.com

....

For more information about
AMBASSADOR INTERNATIONAL
please visit:

www.ambassador-international.com
@AmbassadorIntl
www.facebook.com/AmbassadorIntl